• MOSES PERRY – 1714 - 1801

• A Founding Father of Yarmouth, Nova Scotia

▪ by Mary Ann Mitchell

3RD REVISED EDITION 2016

2745 Laguna Way, Sparks, NV 89434

marymitch2010@gmail.com

Dedicated to
Blanche Firth and Betty Newell
who did so much research for the first edition of
this book.

Table of Contents

CHAPTER 1

INTRODUCTION

The First Settlement of Yarmouth by the English
by Rev. Jonathan Scott*

The town of Yarmouth was inhabited by a few French families before the English inhabited it. The French families settled and lived on the river called Jebogue, or Tebogue, as it is called by some. Their improvements were on and about the hill in Jebogue, and the whole of their improved lands, both the tillage and pasture, exclusive of the marsh, did not exceed one hundred acres. The rest of the land was a wild uncultivated wilderness.

The first families of English that settled in Yarmouth were in the month of June, One Thousand Seven Hundred and Sixty One. The first vefsel that brought settlers brought only three families, which are these, Mr. Moses Perry, Mr. Sealed Landers, and Mr. Ebenezer Ellis. Mr. Landers settled at the head of the river called Cape Forcu or Cape Fursue, as it is called; the other two families settled in Jebogue and these three families came from Mafsachusetts Province. Soon after these, there came a vefsel from Connecticut Colony, which brought a number of families to settle, most of which sat down in Jebogue, among which were Mr. Jonathan Crosby, and Mr. Joshua Burgess. Some of the families that came in the last mentioned vefsel, returned back in a few years after they came, but all the names mentioned above, tarried with their wives and children.

- taken from the beginning page of *'The Records of the Church of Jebogue in Yarmouth'.*

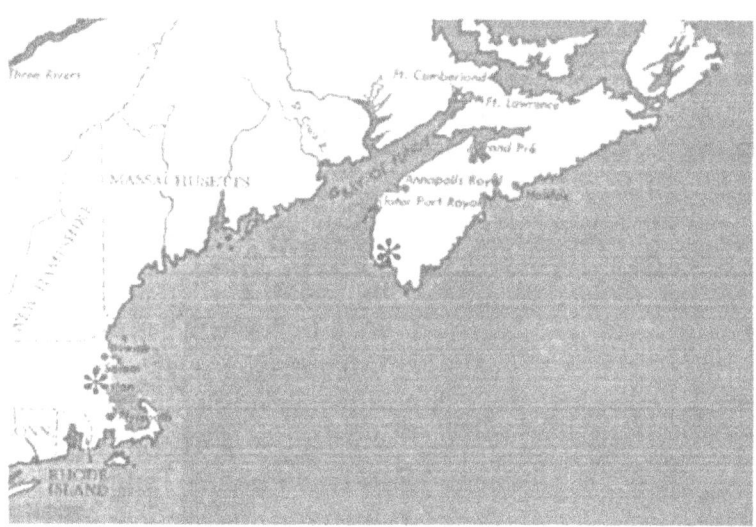

Map of the Eastern Seaboard showing the relationship of
Sandwich, Mass. to Yarmouth, N.S.

.

3

Moses Perry and the Founding of Yarmouth

During the mid-1700's, Moses Perry lived in Sandwich, Massachusetts with his wife Eleanor (Ellis) and their six children. Conditions in Massachusetts at this time in history were becoming somewhat strained, both politically and economically. The farms in Massachusetts were becoming smaller as fathers sub-divided their lands among their children. Also at this time, relations with Great Britain were becoming tense and many people were torn between loyalties to their "motherland" and their more recent home on the west side of the Atlantic.

Many people in Massachusetts looked to Nova Scotia which had been a 'hot bed' of British activity for a decade or more. In 1749, Halifax had been founded and many New Englanders took an interest in the new British settlement. The British Parliament was pouring large amounts of money into the colony and so carpenters and masons came to build, merchants came to open stores, and even a printer brought his printing press with him to start a newspaper. *(from* **Fair Domain** *by George E. Tait)*

In 1755, the Acadians were expelled from Nova Scotia leaving land which had been cultivated for more than a hundred years and *"never failed of crops, nor needed manuring"*. Governor Lawrence of Nova Scotia issued the Charter of Nova Scotia which offered free land (Acadian land) to any "Loyal subject of the King". As a result of the Governor's offer, a substantial number of New Englanders moved to Nova Scotia.

Another attraction for settlers was that southern Nova Scotia was approximately 400 miles closer to the Grand Banks fishing grounds than were their ports in Massachusetts. For many, the once temporary fishing outposts of Nova Scotia, now became their permanent homes. And the political problems in Nova Scotia had become stabilized after the British took Louisburg in 1758. Between 1760 and 1775, the population of Nova Scotia jumped from 2000 to 18,000 persons, the majority being from New England.

In 1761, the Perry Family, with two neighbors from Sandwich, left Massachusetts in a 25-ton shallop named *Pompey Dick*. The 17 people sailed eight days out of Sandwich and landed in Yarmouth on Tuesday June 9, 1761.

1986 - Re-enactment of the Pompey Dick sailing into the Chebogue River

The Perrys and the Ellis' settled along the shores of the Chebogue River where there was good farming land and where the salt marshes provided winter feed for their animals. The Perrys received a grant of 623 acres of land which had been an Acadian orchard. This land was located near the present day corner of the Wyman and Chebogue Roads and descendents, the Walter Perry Family, still live on part of the original family farm. The Landers settled in an area where a lake (now named Milo) flowed into Yarmouth Harbour and here they set up a grist mill. The original grinding stone may still be seen near this site.

The first winter came quickly and took the families off guard. They had brought some supplies with them as well as oxen, cows, calves, hogs and horses. But, they were awaiting the return of the Pompey Dick with more supplies. It never returned leaving the new inhabitants without food and four feet of snow in the area. But, the local First Nation – the Mi'kmaq supplied the families with eels and moose meat that they either traded or sold. For the most part, this commerce kept the struggling settlers alive. – *from Ken Langille's History of Yarmouth 1761-1775*

Moses and Eleanor have the distinction of having the first English child born in the newly founded Yarmouth Township. A daughter, Anna, was born September 6, 1761 which means Eleanor was 6 months pregnant when she sailed on the Pompey Dick. Passed down through the Perry generations is an interesting tale which states that Anna was born under an apple tree on the family farm. This family legend may be based in fact, since *Campbell's History* states that for the family's first dwelling on their new land, Moses spread tenting material over an apple tree on the farm.

The Perry family continued to grow with the births of Elisha in 1765, Levi in 1766 and Samuel in 1769. In 1770, a visiting clergyman from Massachusetts baptized these children who had been born in this new land. The records at the Chebogue Church indicate:

> *"Jebogue June 3, 1770 - Anna, Samuel, Elisha, Levi, children of Mr. Moses Perry, a member of the Church of Christ in Sandwich were baptized by me, Solomon Reed, Pastor of a Church in Middleborough, New England".*

Only one year after the younger children were baptized, Eleanor Perry was taken ill and on November 29, 1771, she died at the age of 46. Rev. Jonathan Scott documents this tragic event in his Journal:

> *"October ye 17, 1771. This day has been observed as a day of fasting and prayer, at Mr. Moses Perry's house in Jebogue. The occasion of this fast, was, on account of Mrs. Perry, who was in a weak and poor state of body, and mind too. She was bereaved of her senses in some measure; and this was introdused by a disponding, disparing state of mind; she told me often, there was no hope of her obtaining mercy from God for her soul, for the day of grace was over with her; and her mind being thus empressed, she would not consent that I should pray with, or for her, though I often prayed with her, but not at her desire or consent."*

> *"December ye 2, 1771. I attended the funeral of Mrs. Perry to-day, who departed this life the 29th of November last. She never came out of her*

dispairing frame till she left the world, as I could learn. She was a professor of Christianity in New England, and a peaceable blameless woman among us, so far as I knoe; and though her sun sat in a cloud here, I hope it is well for her now."

Eleanor Perry was laid to rest in Town Point Cemetery, which is situated near their original landing site. Thirty years later, Moses was buried at her side. Also buried in Town Point Cemetery were their daughter, Anna, and her husband, Silas Clements, as well as another founding father, Ebenezer Ellis and his wife, Hannah., The third member of the original 'Pompey Dick' crew, Sealed Landers, who did not stay in Chebogue, but instead operated a grist mill at the end of Lake Milo in the area which would become Yarmouth North or better known as Milton (Mill Town). Sealed and Thankful Landers were buried in unmarked graves in Yarmouth North.

On the stonewall which surrounds Town Point Cemetery, a plaque has been placed to honour the landing of these first three English speaking families who are known as the 'Founders of Yarmouth'. This plaque reads:

"This tablet commemorates the landing of the first English speaking settlers of Yarmouth near this spot on June 9th, 1761"

The Moses Perry Family Tree:

There is much debate and many, many discrepancies on the early Perry ancestors. Most of the debate centers around Edmund (g.g. grandfather of Moses). The records become well documented starting with Edmund's son, Ezra I, especially when he reached Massachusetts.

Edmund's parents are the first debatable question. Some records state his father was 'John' from London. The rest of the records say Edmund's father was 'Henry' (Henrici) from Devon. Henry's dates and location in England are more in line with what we know of Edmund, but there are no more Henrys in the family and that is unusual as sons were often named after fathers. Another record combines these facts that Edmund's father was John Henrici Perry born in London in 1562 and died in Bridford, Devon in 1622. *(Mary Edmons-Maier Family Tree-Ancestry.com)* Edmund's mother was Richarda Platyr.

Edmund's birth date is another matter in question. So many claims have been registered without thought or proof reading and these mistakes have perpetuated through the years. For example, some records say Edmund was baptized in 1596, but also say he wasn't born until 1598/99. Other records say he died in 1614 which means he fathered eight children after his death! Whether Edmund was still living when the family emigrated to North America is another question. Elwell Perry in his book *Perry-Long Genealogy 1646-1976* states that Sarah (Edmund's wife) was a widow when she arrived in Massachusetts. Other reports say Edmund moved his family to Lynn, Massachusetts and later to Sandwich in 1637. The *Passenger & Immigration Index 1500s to 1900s* states that in 1637, landing in Plymouth, Massachusetts was Edward Perry accompanied by his brother Ezra and mother Sarah.

A list of Perry ancestors is given below but until we have more proof, this list is for interest only. Because of all the uncertainty about our ancestors, in this book, we have started the numbering of generations with Edmund when the information can be verified.

The earliest known Perry in the Moses line according to Jacob M. Price's *Perry of London* hailed from the Devon, England area.

1. **WILLIAM PERRYE** I- born in 1495. He resided in Water, Devon, England. He had two sons: **William II** and **Roger.**
2. **ROGER PERRYE**- born in 1515 - son of William I. In 1532, he was residing in Exeter, Devon, England. Roger was admitted a freeman of Exeter by apprenticeship and later he became a merchant in Exeter. Roger married **Lady Margery PARR** and had two sons: **William III** and **Richard.**
3. **WILLIAM JOHN PERRYE III**- (1540-1590) - son of Roger. In 1560, William was a merchant in Exeter, Devon, England. He imported raisins, figs and wine, presumably from Spain and the Mediterranean. He, along with his brother, are specifically named as merchants trading to Spain and Portugal and as founding members in Queen Elizabeth's charter of 1577 incorporating the Spanish Company. In 1578, he was made bailiff of Exeter. William married **Lady Jane HOLCOMBE** (daughter of John) from Plymouth, England. They had **Edmund, William IV,** and **Henry (Henrici).**

4. HENRICI (HENRY) PERRYE (born 1564/65) - son of William III. He was christened in St. Mary Major in Exeter. In 1587, he was residing in Buckland Monachorum, Devon which is a few miles north of Plymouth. He was a merchant in the import/export business with a suggestion that it could have been in cloth. There is no record of him owning real estate. On June 12, 1587, he married **RICHARDA PLATYR (**born 1567) from Buckland Monachorum. They had **William V, Thomas, Henry** and **Edmund.**

(this early family information from Jacob M. Price's 'Perry of London')

AUTHOR'S NOTES: 1. Some references name **John** *- born in 1562 in London as Edmund's father. However, from An Incomplete History of the Descendents of John Perry of London by Bertram Adams, it is stated that the John Perry descendents who came to North America did so in 1666. We know Ezra was here by 1637. Also the book states that John's grandsons were John, Josiah and Joseph, all names not associated with the Ezra line. So for these reasons, John as the father of Edmund was rejected.*

2. There is a very comprehensive DNA study being conducted on the Perry Family. The males who were tested submitted their genealogy information (as they knew it). The results show that the known Ezra descendents are closely related to one test who claims to be related to a Richard Perry, born 1580 and his son Roger. So it is very evident that there is still a lot of work to be done on Edmund's ancestors.

3. A name with a superscript number indicates the generation number starting with Edmund Perry who was the first well documented Perry of this line.

4. An underlined name in a family listing indicates that this individual will be discussed in more detail later in the book.

5. As you are reading through the families, notice the very high portion of twins born into this Perry Tree.

6. Many of the contributors of this book included birthdates for all family members. I do appreciate this knowing the extra work it took . But because of the time we live in, it was thought more prudent to exclude the birth dates of the living generations.

7. Electronic versions of this book are also available.

8. Realizing a work of this size will contain errors, I would appreciate being notified of any errors or additions, so that the record for future generations will be as accurate as possible. Mary Ann – e-mail – marymitch2010@gmail.com

Early Perry History

St. Mary Major - A small parish in the old walled City of Exeter, just inside the West Gate, where Henry Perrye was christened in 1565.

"St. Mary Major Church is in West Street, at the foot of Stepcote hill, adjoining the site of the West gate, through which the city was formerly entered by a flight of steps. It is a small ancient fabric, and in its tower is a curious clock, over the dial of which are three small figures:- the centre one representing Henry VIII, in a sitting posture, bends forward every time the clock strikes; and the other two are in military costume, with javelins in their right hands, and in their left small hammers, with which they alternately strike the quarters on two small bells beneath their feet".

[From White's Devonshire Directory (1850)]

Stepcote Hill Steps with St Mary Major Church on left corner

1.**EDMUND PERRY**— son of **Henry OR John**, was born 27 January, 1588/89 in Buckland Monachorum, Devon, England and christened there the same year.

On October 2, 1613, Edmund married **SARAH BETTS CROWELL** *(Church of LDS-Ancestral File, June 1998)* in Bridford, Devon. Sarah was born 1592 in London, England - died in Sandwich, Massachusetts on June 8,1659, *(**ref: Perry Family freepages genealogy; Teague Roots & Branches.**)* She was the daughter of John and Elisha Crowell. Edmund's family immigrated to Plymouth, Massachusetts in the 1630s. It is generally thought Edmund had died prior to the arrival. From Plymouth, the family moved to Sandwich, Massachusetts in June, 1637 *(Virkus, p.54) (Sandwich Historical Society).* The sons of the family were: **Arthur, Anthony, John, William VI, Ezra, Edward.**

2. **EZRA PERRY I (**born in 1625 and died 16 October, 1689)— born in Devon, England, son of Edmund and Sarah—married **ELIZABETH BURGES (Burgess)** (born 1629, near Truro, Cornwall, England - died 26 September, 1717). She was the daughter of Thomas and Dorothy (Phippen-Waynes) Burges from England. Ezra and Elizabeth had 7 children.

3. **EZRA PERRY II** (born 11 February,1652/53 in Sandwich, Massachusetts and died 31 January, 1729/30) —son of Ezra and Elizabeth—married **REBECCA FREEMAN** in 1673. Rebecca (born 1650-died 16 April, 1738) was the daughter of Edmond and Rebecca (Prence) Freeman, whose grandfather, William Brewster, came over on the Mayflower, and whose father,Thomas Prence, was governor of Plymouth Colony. Ezra and Rebecca had 8 children.

4. **SAMUEL PERRY** (born 20 March, 1687/88 and died in 1730)—son of Ezra II and Rebecca—married **SARAH LEONARD** in 1710. Sarah was the daughter of Solomon and Mary Leonard of Middleborough, Massachusetts. Samuel and Sarah had 6 children.

5 . **MOSES PERRY**(1714-1801)—son of Samuel and Sarah—in 1743, married **ELEANOR ELLIS** (1725-1771). Eleanor was the daughter of Gideon and Ann (Clark) Ellis. Moses and Eleanor moved from Sandwich, Massachusetts to Chebogue, Yarmouth, Nova Scotia in 1761. They had 11 children.

These 11 children of Moses and Eleanor Perry were:

1. **Prence**—born 3 November, 1744
2. **Rebecca**—born 19 March, 1748
3. **Sarah**—born 27 May, 1750
4. **Moses**—born 30 August 1752; died prior to 1761
5. **Thomas**—born 4 May, 1755
6. **Joseph**—born 7 November, 1756
7. **Nathaniel**—born 24 June, 1759
8. **Anna**—born 6 September, 1761
9. **Elisha**—born in 1765
10. **Levi**—born in 1766
11. **Samuel** – born March 1769

The Commonwealth of Massachusetts

UNITED STATES OF AMERICA.

COPY OF RECORD OF BIRTH

Town of Sandwich

I, the undersigned, hereby certify that I am clerk of the Town of Sandwich that as such I have custody of the records of births required by law to be kept in my office; that among such records is one relating to the birth of

Samuel Perry

and that the following is a true copy of so much of said record as relates to said birth, namely:

Date of Birth 20th day of March XXXXX Anno Domini 1688

Place of Birth Sandwich

Name of Child Samuel Perry

Sex Son Color

FATHER	MOTHER
Name Ezra Perry	Name (Maiden) Rebecca his wife
Residence Sandwich	Residence Sandwich
Place of Birth	Place of Birth
Occupation	Occupation

Date of Record Date of Amendment

And I do hereby certify that the foregoing is a true copy from said records.

Witness my hand and seal of said Town of Sandwich on this seventeenth day of March 19 86

SEAL

Barbara J. Walling   Clerk

Year 1679-1815
Vol. 2
Page 29
No.

11

The Commonwealth of Massachusetts

UNITED STATES OF AMERICA.

COPY OF RECORD OF BIRTH

Town   nf   Sandwich

I, the undersigned, hereby certify that I am clerk of the ....Town........ of ....Sandwich........

that as such I have custody of the records of births required by law to be kept in my office; that among such records is one relating to the birth of

................................Moses Perry................................

and that the following is a true copy of so much of said record as relates to said birth, namely:

Date of Birth........20th day of December xxxx Anno Domini 1714

Place of Birth ....Sandwich

Name of Child........Moses Perry

Sex........Son........Color ....

FATHER	MOTHER
Name ....Samuel Perry Junr.	Name (Maiden) ..Sarah his wife..........
Residence........Sandwich	Residence ....Sandwich
Place of Birth........	Place of Birth........
Occupation	Occupation ....

Date of Record .... Date of Amendment ....

And I do hereby certify that the foregoing is a true copy from said records.

Witness my hand and seal of said ....Town....of....Sandwich........

on this........seventeenth........day of........March........1986

SEAL

12

Perry Personality Glimpses

Ezra Perry I
Great-Grandfather of Moses Perry

These well preserved tombstones shown below are still standing in the old graveyard behind the Sandwich, Massachusetts' town hall.

-photos courtesy of Lewis Perry

Ezra Perry I (son of Edmund) moved to Sandwich with his parent(s) when he was 12 years old. *"He {Ezra} was one of the party that came to Sandwich in June 1637"* (*Sandwich Historical Society*).

Ezra served in the militia as a Lieutenant and was a constable of Sandwich. He and Elizabeth had seven children.

Ezra's will made on 16 October, 1689 after providing that his body be buried *"at ye ordinary place of burring"*, disposes of his estate as follows:

> *"All my outward moveables, with out doars and within docars to my truly*
> *and well beloved wife, as my true undoubted and lawful executrix, to*
> *dispose of at her pleasure excepting what I shall leave and bequeath.-*
> *-I leave and bequeathe to my well beloved son, Samuel, 2 stiers of two, and one*
> *heifer of four years and a mare coult; one bed and furniture... gune and sword*
> *and ban daleers and one iron pot.*
> *-To my well beloved son Benjamin Perry two cowes, two steeres about*
> *three years old, one bed and its furniture, one gune ,one sword*
> *-To my daughter Remember two cowes, one bed and its furniture, one*
> *meare and her increase*
> *-Also to my son Ezra one shilling*
> *-To John Perry my son one shilling*
> *-Deborah my daughter wife of Seth Pope one shilling*
> *-To Sarah wife of Ephraim Swift one shilling."*

Ezra Perry II
Grandfather of Moses Perry

Some time in the 1670's, Ezra, along with his brothers, Samuel, John, and Benjamin, built a house along the South Bank of the Monument River in Massachusetts. A story was told of how they would come home at night, take refuge behind a large rock in front of the house, and fire several volleys of gunfire into the house before entering. This was done to scare away any indians that may be lurking in the house.

Ezra's brother Samuel (1667-1751) kept a tavern in Bourne, Massachusetts. Relics from this tavern are preserved by the Historical Society there. Some of Samuel's descendents married into the Francis Cook Family (of Mayflower Fame), as did Ezra's, and one of the descendents was President Franklin Delano Roosevelt.

Brother John (1657-1732) lived along the Monument all his life and the house stood until 1794 when it burnt down. John was a yeoman farmer and a descendent of his was P.T. Barnum of circus fame.

Brother Benjamin's family moved to Vermont. His son Abner was *"killed in action during the siege of Louisburg on Cape Breton Island"* and son Nathaniel raised a company to *"remove the French encroachments from His Majesty's Government in Nova Scotia, where he died in service at the age of 44" (Wight, p.40).*

A Mr. Thomas, Genealogical Editor of the Connecticut Quarterly, states that this Ezra had a wife before Rebecca Freeman and they had Ebenezer, Mary and Bethiah. *(This can not be verified by this author).* Ezra II (1652-31 January, 1729) married Rebecca Freeman (1650-16 April,1738) who brought family money into the marriage.

Ezra managed to buy up tracts of land in Plymouth County and he swore the "Oath of Fidelity" in 1678. It was reported that Ezra Perry administered his father-in-law's (Edmond Freeman) estate. It would appear from accounts that Ezra had to bring a suit against his brother-in-law in order to retain the estate in his hands.

Ezra's will left Rebecca the use and improvement of all real and personal estate. Son Ebenezer received all meadows and swampy meadows in Rochester, and Ezra III, the eldest, got *"all the land before my dwelling."* It is known that son Samuel owned considerable land in Sandwich, but it is not known if this was bequeathed from his father, or if Samuel acquired the land on his own.

Samuel Perry
Father of Moses Perry

Samuel was born 20 March, 1688 in Sandwich, Barnstable, Massachusetts to Ezra II and Rebecca. On December 14, 1710, he married Sarah Leonard, daughter of Solomon and Mary (Trasher) Leonard. Sarah was born 1688 in Barnstable, Massachusetts and died Oct. 1735 in Sandwich. Samuel died August 3, 1756 in Rehoboth, Bristol Co. Massachusetts, before Moses sailed for Nova Scotia.

A Look into the Personality of Moses Perry

The Chebogue Church Records (p. 120-122) give us an insight into what beliefs and convictions Moses Perry had.

Moses, along with Rev. Jonathan Scott, brought a complaint in front of the Church against a Mr. Seth Barnes for using *"Prophaneness of Speech"* and for *"Breach of the Sabbath"*.

On 19th of September, 1779, Mr. Barnes was on a vessel which was boarded by a Captain Allerdice, Commander of the Buckran. In the King's name, Captain Allerdice seized some pitch and tar which were under the care of Mr. Barnes. In response to this and in the presence of Moses and Rev. Scott, Seth Barnes uttered this phrase, *"What the Devil does he mean by this?"* And then to make matters worse, one week later on Sunday, the 26th of September, Mr. Barnes bargained and sold a yoke of oxen.

> *"Friday, October ye 22, 1779. We the subscribers being together with Capt. Seth Barnes, endeavoured to convince him of his Sin, namely Prophaneness of Speech and Breach of Sabbath, ...and to bring him to a due Sense and Repentance therefor; but without Success, as Things appeared to us. For though he did not deny the facts to us, yet he appeared remote from any repentance or sorrow for the sin thereof. And with Respect to selling his Oxen on the Lord's Day, he said, "If it was to do again, and things were circumstanced as they then were, and he saw things as he then did, he should do the like again".*   *-Moses Perry & Jonathan Scott*

Seth Barnes was then notified in writing to come before the church and answer the charges.

> *Tuesday, June ye 27, 1780. "Mr. Barnes acknowledged the whole of the charge exhibited against him to be true, but did not for some time acknowledge himself faulty in selling his oxen on the Sabbath, but at last he was brought to own and acknowledge that he had dishonoured God and Religion by this Act of selling his oxen on the Sabbath, and also in using prophane speech. And he declared that he was sorry therefor, and that he would strive against the like sins for the future.*
> *Upon hearing these things, the Pastor made the motion and the Church gave their unanimous vote, and forgave and restored Mr. Seth Barnes to their charity."*

The Death Date of Moses Perry

There has been much debate among researchers about the death date of Moses Perry. The majority of sources consulted stated that he died in 1811, while a few said the date was 1801.

When Moses Perry's tombstone was found by Firth and Mitchell in Town Point Cemetery at Chebogue, his death was recorded on 13 November, 1801. This date seemed more likely since Moses would have died at 87 years, instead of 97, which would be an accomplishment for those times. The deciding factor came from an obscure reference found in Jonathan Scott's writings which referred to the *"late Moses Perry"*. This entry was dated 1808.

enhanced photo by M.Mitchell

CHAPTER 2
THE DESCENDENTS OF
PRENCE, REBECCA, MOSES, JOSEPH, and SAMUEL
five of Moses' eleven children

1st child of Moses
PRENCE PERRY[6] (Church records show 'Prince')
son of :   Moses[5], Samuel[4], Ezra[3], Ezra [2], Edmund[1]

BORN: 3 November, 1744 in Sandwich, Massachusetts
DIED: After 1790
MARRIED: 1st **Mercy Cobb** on 13 March, 1772 in Truro, Barnstable, MA; 2nd
                  Deliverance Gross
CHILDREN:
(by Mercy)   1. **Ruth (Perry) Byron[7]**—born 20 July, 1775; records show a
                  guardian being appointed for Ruth in 1783. It is surmised that
                  Prence was most likely away from home during the American
                  Revolutionary War years and Mercy had already died. Ruth
                  married **James Byron** on 10 December, 1804.
(by Deliverance): 2. **Moses Perry[7]**—born September, 1787; married **Lois Collins** on
                  14 June, 1810. Moses and Lois had three children:
                     (1) **Loisa Perry[8]**—born 6 April, 1812.
                     (2) **Joanna Collins Perry[8]**—27 Feb. 1814.
                     (3) **Moses Ellis Perry[8]**—born 1819.
                  3. **Deliverance (Perry) Rich[7]**—born 6 October, 1793;
                     married **Theophilus Rich** on 10 August, 1813. Deliverance died
                     8 July,1837.

> *"Prence, the eldest son of Moses may have been apprenticed (he would*
> *have been 17 years of age) when his parents and younger siblings sailed*
> *for Nova Scotia in 1761. If he did accompany his family there, he didn't*
> *stay long because records show he was living in Truro, Massachusetts at*
> *the time of his first marriage in 1772."*
> *(Ezra Perry of Sandwich, Mass (c. 1625-1689) by Lydia B. (Phinney) Brownson and*
> *MacLean W. MacLean)*

2nd child of Moses
REBECCA (PERRY) ELLIS[6]
daughter of: Moses[5,] Samuel[4], Ezra[3], Ezra[2], Edmund[1]

BORN: 19 March, 1748, in Sandwich, Massachusetts
DIED: 1829.
MARRIED: **Phillip Ellis** (1750-17 April, 1831)(son of Benjamin). Phillip was a
                  sergeant in Capt. Ward Swift's Company during the Revolutionary War.
                  Phillip and Rebecca were married 20 November,1771 and they had 12
                  children.
CHILDREN: 1. **Lois (Ellis) Stubbs[7]**—born 8 October,1772; married **Joseph Stubbs**.

2. **Eleanor (Ellis) Brown, Bootland**[7]—born 14 May 1774
married: 1st **George Duron Brown** 21 Feb. 1793; 2nd **Capt. Bootland**
(son of George) on 26 November,1800.
3. **Remembrance (Ellis) Baker**[7]—born 23 Nov. 1775; married **Edward Baker** (son of Jonathan I).
4. **Herman Ellis**[7]—born 27 June,1777.
5. *Joseph Ellis*[7]—born 10 March,1779, died 29 Dec. 1851.
6. **Moses Ellis**[7]—born 17 November,1780.
7. **Watson Ellis**[7]—born 21 October,1782.
8. **Sarah & Anna Ellis**[7] (twins) —born 20 Sept. 1784.
9. **Thomas Ellis**[7] —born 11 July1787.
10. **Alden Ellis**[7]—born 15 November,1789.
11. **Phillip Ellis**[7]—born 17 November,1792.

JOSEPH ELLIS[7] *(reportedly brought up by his Aunt Anna (Perry)Clements)*
son of: Rebecca (Perry) Ellis[6], Moses[5], Samuel[4], Ezra[3], Ezra[2],Edmund[1]

BORN: 10 March,1779.

Capt. Silas Clements, who had married Anna Perry (Rebecca's sister) had no son of their own, so they urged Phillip and Rebecca Ellis to let them have one of their 12 children. Joseph went to live with them when he was 8 years old. He was brought back to Chebogue, where he lived with his aunt and uncle until he came of age, receiving such advantages as the common school afforded, in addition to special home instruction. Capt. Clements took him to sea at an early age so that Joseph Ellis became a Master Mariner by age 21. From that time on, he followed the sea, sailing to all parts of the world that vessels usually visited at that period. Meanwhile he did not neglect his studies, so we find him teaching school during the winter seasons at Chebogue and at the Cove, and at a later date one or more terms at Ohio, Nova Scotia.

  Joseph Ellis did not become especially active in religious matters until 1814, but from that time forward he became zealous in his work, was broad minded and progressive in home missionary and temperance matters, frequently making house-to-house visitations and he was at all times, whether in public or in private, ready to show, both by percept and example, his spiritual fellowship.
  -from George S. Brown's Yarmouth, Nova Scotia Genealogies, p. 104-105.

MARRIED: **Ruth Porter** (daughter of Nehemiah J. and Mary (Tardy) Porter) on 8 January, 1802. Ruth was born 9 December,1782, and died 3 September, 1865. Both Joseph Ellis and Ruth are buried in Town Point Cemetery.
DIED: 29 December,1851.
CHILDREN: 1.**Joseph Alden Ellis**[8]—born 10 March, 1803; married **Elizabeth Haley** (daughter of Oliver) 26 Jan. 1826. Elizabeth died in 1887. They are buried in Mountain Cemetery in Yarmouth.

Joseph Alden followed the sea at intervals from 1815 to 1821, fishing, voyages to the United States and West Indies, attending school in winter seasons. From 1821 to 1825, he sailed on larger vessels to South America and Europe, returning to Yarmouth as mate of the Royal Oak in 1825. He was offered a master's berth but preferred to remain at home, marry and settle down in life. (Geo. Brown p.106)

2. **Loran DeWolf Ellis**[8]—born 4 November, 1804; married **Miss Rulmon** (daughter of Colonel Christian of Virginia); second **Malinda Price,** (daughter of James of Carlisle, Indiana).

In October 1822, Loran moved to Springfield, Massachusetts with his uncle. He accompanied his uncle through western Massachusetts and New York State selling such goods as were then common in country stores. In September, they went south as far as Virginia, where they traded till the following May, when Lorne engaged in similar business on his own account. He married a daughter of Colonel Christian Rulmon of Pendleton County, Virginia. She died about two years later and Loran went to the Western States where he married a second time. Loran and his wife died in Missouri.

From *(Geo. Brown p. 107)*

3. **George Colin Ellis**[8]—born 10 September,1812; died 22 August 1814.
4. **Althea Ann (Ellis) Messenger**[8]—born 26 May, 1817; married **Samuel Messenger** (son of David of Annapolis) on 14 Nov. 1833. Althea died 1904.
5. **George Colin Ellis**[8]—born 17 November, 1819; died 24 Aug.1827 .

4th child of Moses
MOSES PERRY[6]
son of: Moses[5], Samuel[4], Ezra[3], Ezra[2], Edmund[1]

BORN: 30 August, 1752 in Sandwich, Massachusetts.
DIED: prior to 1761.

6th child of Moses
JOSEPH PERRY[6]
son of: Moses[5], Samuel[4], Ezra[3], Ezra[2], Edmund[1]*

BORN: 7 November, 1756 in Sandwich, Massachusetts, and baptized there.
DIED: circa 1804.
Although very little is known of Joseph, Lydia (Phinney) Brownson states:
"There is some reason to believe this son matured and had issue."
(Ezra Perry of Sandwich, Mass (c. 1625-1689)).

11th child of Moses
SAMUEL PERRY
son of: Moses[5], Samuel[4], Ezra[3], Ezra[2], Edmund[1]

BORN: March 1769 in Chebogue, Nova Scotia
MARRIED: **Nellie Allener** (born in 1775) on 10 March 1798
Not much is known of Samuel, except a report that he was a member of a company of Royal Fusiliers.

Town Point, as the name implies, was initially the intended site for the new town. However, the town grew alongside the two mile long harbor of Yarmouth instead.

-------------Campbell's History p. 188

By the mid-1800's, a surge for more and faster ships occurred. The Australian and Californian gold rushes, the Crimean War, the mutiny in India, Europe's Industrial Revolution and the American Civil War all added to the flood of people and goods that had to be carried around the world.

Yarmouth had been building small ships for years but after 1852, ships over 1000 tons began to appear. The Yarmouth ship builders began to realize that it would be more profitable to keep and operate the ships they built. By 1876, Yarmouth's population was slightly less than 6,000 and yet these people owned 282 ships. Yarmouth at this time had a tonnage more than 80 times greater than that of Liverpool, England. Yarmouth became rich. Some twenty shipyards were operating in Yarmouth at this time. By the late 1880s, the little town that Moses founded was the fourth largest port of registry in the world!

1802, Yarmouth's Dr. J.N. Bond received some cowpox vaccine from his brother in England, who in turn received the experimental vaccine from his close friend, Dr. Edward Jenner.

Dr. Bond used the vaccine on an infant who was only a few weeks old. The vaccine was effective, and as a final proof of the value of the vaccine, Dr. Bond inoculated the child with smallpox. The child did not become infected and actually lived to a ripe old age.

Dr. Bond was certainly the first doctor to use a vaccination against smallpox in Yarmouth, possibly the first in Nova Scotia and among the first on the North American continent.

----------------Campbell's 'History of Yarmouth County' p. 94.

One hundred years ago, your forefathers left their loved and happy homes in New England to plant on this soil the flag that waves above you ...To that flag which they brought with them, flying from the mast of the little 'Pompey', your fathers adhered through good report and evil report."

--------------------From a Speech given by Dr. G.F. Farish on the occasion of Yarmouth's Centennial – 1861

CHAPTER 3
DESCENDENTS OF SARAH (PERRY) BAIN

3rd child of Moses
SARAH (PERRY) BAIN[6]
daughter of: Moses[5], Samuel[4], Ezra[3], Ezra[2], Edmund[1]

BORN: 27 May, 1750 in Sandwich, Massachusetts.
MARRIED: **Alexander Bain** (son of Alexander and Beulah) on 2 Dec. 1774.
             They had 10 children. Alexander's second wife was **Elizabeth Scott**
             (daughter of Moses) and they had 5 children. Alexander died on 2 April,
             1831.
DIED: circa 1804.

A Family story has survived about Sarah and Alexander- courtesy of Bonnie (Perry) Healy
"Sarah Perry, young daughter of Moses Perry, was sitting by the shore of the Chebogue River one summer day. Her father, on his way to the shore, noticed Sarah sitting there looking out to sea. He asked her what she was doing. She said she was watching for a young man to come in from the sea who would be her husband. They laughed together as she was only 9 years old. Sometime the following year, Alexander Bain was put ashore in Chebogue after being picked up at sea from a ship wreck which claimed his parents and sister. Alexander was raised by John MacKinnon and a few years later, Alexander asked Moses for his daughter's hand in marriage. Moses Perry then told Alexander the story of Sarah watching the sea at nine years of age".

"Yarmouth December y2, 1774. This day, Mr. Alexander Bain and Miss Sarah Perry, both of the town of Yarmouth, were married, after lawful publishment, by me" –J. Scott

Alexander Bain – courtesy of Nate Bain
Alexander Bain was born in Scotland and in 1762 while immigrating to North America with his parents and sister, they were shipwrecked off the port of St. John. Alexander, who was 8 years old at the time, survived by clinging to a mast. His parents and sister did not survive. Alexander was rescued by John MacKinnon of Yarmouth and brought home and raised by the MacKinnon Family.

Alexander became a successful landowner. He owned land on both sides of Yarmouth's current Prospect Street (which was known as the Granny Bain Road) and on the west side of Main Street-Prospect to Hibernia. The land on the south side of Prospect Street was sold to Mr. B. Goudey who later sold it to the Town of Yarmouth for a reservoir to hold a water supply from Lake George. Alexander Bain also owned farmland in Hebron at the Scotts Road area; a large wood lot around Bind Lake and considerable dyke land. Alexander left most of his property to daughter, Barbara and son, John.

The Bain surname is a Gaelic word meaning 'white' or 'beautiful' and when applied to a mountain, it means 'snow capped'. The Bains (various spellings McBain, Ben, Ban, Beann, Bainn, Bean, or Bane), were the people who lived among snow capped mountains. They are considered to be a branch of the clan MacIntosh.

CHILDREN of SARAH AND ALEXANDER:

1. **Barbara (Bain) Ely**[7]—born 19 November, 1775; married **Elijah Ely** on 30 June, 1794. The couple was married by Rev. Jonathan Scott, as were her parents.

2. **Alexander Bain II**[7]—born 28 September,1776; married **Bethia Brown** (daughter of James).

3. **Moses Bain**[7]—born 2 April, 1779; married **Sarah**; Moses was lost at sea in 1805.

4. **John E. Bain**[7]—born 10 March,1781; died 1867; married **Sarah Landers** (daughter of Jabez). John and Sarah had 6 children:.

   (1) **John Bain**[8]—born 26 August,1804; married **Matilda Flint** (daughter of Capt. David).

   (2) **Barbara Bain**[8]—born 10 October,1806.

   (3) **Samuel Soames Bain**[8]—born 1 November,1808; married **Harriet Goudey** (daughter of Soames Benjamin). Samuel Soames and Harriet had 2 children:

      (i) **Sarah (Bain) DeWolfe**[9]—born 31 January, 1837; married **Capt. Charles DeWolfe** (son of Simon) .

      (ii) **Norman B. Bain**[9]—born 1845, died 1877.

   (4) **Eleanor (Bain) Moses**[8]—born 3 May,1810; married **Cyrus Moses** (son of John) on 3 May, 1840.

   (5) **Eunice (Bain) Porter**[8]—born 1812; married **Enoch Porter** (son of Benjamin) on 13 May, 1838; Eunice died 6 December,1838.

   (6) **Joseph Bain**[8]—died unmarried.

5. **Sarah (Bain) Lovitt**[7]—born 20 January,1783; died 21 May 1831; married **Israel Lovitt** (son of Andrew) on 13 January, 1803. Sarah and Israel had 10 children:

   (1) **Andrew Lovitt** [8]— born 23 Nov. 1803, married **Elizabeth Hunter** (daughter of George) on 9 March,1826. Second he married **Abigail L. Pinkney**, (daughter of John) on 5 Nov. 1865.

   (2) **Sarah (Lovitt) MacKenzie**[8]—born 23 January, 1805; married **Daniel MacKenzie**; Sarah died 16 May, 1828.

   (3) **Capt. Israel Lovitt**[8]—born 13 May, 1807; married **Elizabeth B. Ring** (daughter of Lemuel) on 7 February, 1832; Israel was lost at sea February,1841. Israel and Elizabeth had a son:

      (i) **Thomas B. Lovitt (Capt)**[9]—married **Harriet E. Bain** (daughter of James Brown) *(see page 28)* on 2 March, 1867. Capt. Thomas was lost at sea in November,1869. They had one daughter:

a). **Annie M. Bolton (Lovitt) Horton**[10] — was born 10
   November,1868, died 20 Dec. 1944. She married **Edward
   Allen Horton** (son of Dennis).

(4) **John Walker Lovitt**[8] —born 20 June, 1809; married **Anne
   Jenkins** (daughter of James); John died 14 July,1874.

(5) **Joseph Lovitt**[8]—born 8 Mar. 1812; married 1st **Elizabeth P.
   Goudey** (daughter of George) on 11 October, 1837; 2nd married
   Anne Maria Gunnhill (of Shropshire, England) on 6 June, 1842.
   Joseph died 1 September, 1888.

(6) **Henry Lovitt**[8]—born 26 December,1813; lost at sea 1841;
   unmarried.

(7) **Obadiah Wilson Lovitt**[8]—born 16 February, 1816; died 27
   August,1841 in Demerora, South America; unmarried.

(8) **Mary E. (Lovitt) Porter**[8]—born 24 November,1818;
   married **Capt. Horace B. Porter** (son of Ebenezer) on 26
   February, 1839; died 7 March, 1873.

(9) **Lydia Anne (Lovitt) Murphy**[8]—born 5 March, 1821;
   married **Capt. Benjamin Murphy** (son of James) on
   20 February, 1840.

(10) **Alexander Bain Lovitt**[8]-born 25 Sept. 1823; married **Maria
   Taylor** (daughter of George from Weymouth) on 5 June, 1855.
   Alexander died 3 Feb. 1897.

6. <u>**Samuel Bain**</u>[7]—born 14 November,1785; died 14 Sept.,1850;
   married 1st **Eunice Landers** (daughter of Capt. Jabez); 2nd
   Hannah Kelley (daughter of Capt. James).

7 <u>**William Bain**</u> [7]—born 10 April, 1787; married **Asenath Porter**
   (daughter of Hasadiah).

8. **Joseph Bain**[7]—born on 9 February,1788; married **Mary Corning**
   (daughter of David). Mary was born 14 August,1785. Joseph died 10
   November,1852. Mary and Joseph had 3 children:

   (1) **Mary (Bain) Crocker**[8]—married **Capt. Wendall Crocker**
      (son of Joseph). They adopted the daughter of David Parry and
      for many years provided a home for Joseph Walker Corning after
      the devastating Beaver River fire.*(from the Joseph Walker
      Corning's letters.)*

   (2) **Elijah Bain**[8]—married **Miss Cashenbury** (daughter of Peter).

   (3) **Roxanna (Bain) Phillips**[8]—married **James Phillips** (son of
      Capt. John T.).

9. **Eleanor (Bain) Dodge, Porter**[7]—born 13 September,1792;
   married 1st **William Dodge**; 2nd **Benjamin Porter** (son of Josiah)
   on 20 September,1830. Eleanor died 2 Aug. 1865. Eleanor had 6
   children—3 by William and 3 by Benjamin:

(by William)

   (1) **William Dodge**[8] —unmarried.

   (2) **Nancy (Dodge) Robertson**[8]—married **William
      Robertson.**

   (3) **Leah (Dodge) Doty**[8]—married **Chipman P. Doty** (son of
      William); died 24 April,1895.

23

(by Benjamin)

(4) **Charles Porter**[8]—born 29 November,1832; married **May A. Canning** (daughter of Charles) on 20 July,1867.

(5) **George H. Porter**[8]—born 29 July,1834; married **Elizabeth H. Harris** (daughter of James T.) on 7 Aug. 1858.

(6) **Jane E. (Porter) Perry**[8]—born 13 November,1836; married **Ansel Perry** (son of Miner) on 7 July, 1858.

10. **Anna (Bain) Shaw**[7]—born 27 May, 1795; married **Capt. Joseph Shaw** (son of Joseph). Capt. Joseph died 30 July, 1871. Anna died 22 December,1834. Anna and Joseph had 6 children:

(1) **Joseph Shaw**[8]—married **Letitia Ann Porter** (daughter of Nehemiah) on 22 December, 1842.

(2) **Elizabeth (Shaw) MacKenna**[8]—married **Capt. Jonathan MacKenna** (son of Jonathan).

(3) **Israel Shaw**[8]—lost at sea September, 1843; unmarried.

(4) **Abby Chipman (Shaw) Ryerson**[8]—married **Capt. John K. Ryerson** (son of Stephen D.).

(5) **Silas Clements Shaw**[8]— died in California 28 January, 1862; unmarried. *Silas was undoubtedly named for his Uncle.*

(6) **Anne S. (Shaw) Ryerson**[8]—married **Samuel Ryerson** (son of Stephen) on 5 October,1853; died 3 April, 1898.

1st son of Sarah
ALEXANDER BAIN II[7]
son of: Sarah (Perry) Bain[6], Moses[5], Samuel[4], Ezra[3], Ezra[2], Edmund[1].

BORN: 28 September, 1776.
MARRIED: **Bethia Brown** (daughter of James).
CHILDREN: 1. **Bethia (Bain) Dalton**[8]—born 26 August,1798; Bethia died 13 June, 1851. She married **Maurice Dalton** and they had 6 children:

(1) **Harriet (Dalton) Raymond**[9]—married **Wellsley W. Raymond** (son of John) on 9 October,1842.

(2) **Azor Dalton**[9]—born 1823; died 5 May,1850; unmarried.

(3) **Calvin Dalton**[9]—married **Sarah Cann** (daughter of Elder Calvin Cann).(*see page 26*)

(4) **Maria (Dalton) Stanwood**[9]—married **Capt. Joseph Stanwood** (son of Sam) on 12 February,1854. Maria died 13 October, 1860.

(5) **Melissa Jane (Dalton) Suttie**[9]—married **James E. Suttie** (son of Andrew) on 17 March 1853. Melissa died 25 March,1897.

(6) **Henry Dalton**[9]—born in1837; died 17 October, 1860; unmarried.

2. <u>**Alexander Bain III**</u> [8]—born 14 Sept.1800; married 1st **Martha Rose** (daughter of David) on 1 January,1825. Married 2nd **Edith Harris** (daughter of William) on 20 February, 1834, and 3rd married **Jane Jenkins** (daughter of John) on 13 November, 1836.

3. **Harriet (Bain) Killiam** [8]—born 15 October, 1803; married **Abraham Killiam** (son of Abraham). Harriet and Abraham had 2 children:
   (1) **Lois (Killiam) Richard** [9]—born 1826; married **Capt. Richard** (son of Richard) on 20 July, 1843. Lois died 17 March, 1895.
   (2) **Jacob Killiam** [9]—drowned in California, April 1851; unmarried. *Was he searching for gold like so many others?*

4. **Sarah (Bain) Cann** [8]—born 3 July, 1805; married **Lyman Cann** (son of John) on 22 January, 1825. *The 1838 Nova Scotia census state that Lyman was a carpenter.* After Sarah's death in circa 1846, Lyman married 2nd **Elizabeth Hibbert** (daughter of Rufus) on 24 November, 1853. They had three children and Elizabeth died 17 April, 1864. Sarah and Lyman had 11 children:
   (1) **Lyman Cann** [9]—born 30 November 1825; married **Sarah MacLearn Locke** (daughter of James D. of Locke's Island) on 16 January, 1850. Lyman died 4 January, 1888.
   (2) **Hugh M. Cann** [9]—born 10 October, 1827; married **Joanna H. Lovitt** (daughter of Andrew) *(see p. 22)* on 25 February, 1851.
   (3) **William A. Cann** [9]— born 1 January, 1829.
   (4) **Sarah Jane Cann** [9]—18 April, 1832; died 4 March, 1833.
   (5) **Sarah Jane (Cann) Churchill** [9]—born 26 July, 1833; married **Edison Churchill** (son of Benjamin) on 1 December, 1853. Sarah died 14 February, 1890.
   (6) **Adeline (Cann) Lewis** [9]—born 3 January, 1835; married **Nathan B. Lewis** (son of William) on 11 December, 1855. Adeline died 11 June, 1896.
   (7) **Cecila (Cann) Chipman** [9]—born 26 July, 1838; married **Capt. Thomas D. Chipman** (son of Thomas D.) on 15 December, 1858. Cecila died 1873.
   (8) **Harriet K. (Cann) Tooker** [9]—born 6 April, 1841; married **Capt. George W. B. Tooker** (son of Charles) on 25 Feb. 1864.
   (9) **Angus W. Cann** [9]—born 30 June, 1844; married **Eliza Cann** (daughter of William B.). Angus died 30 July, 1883.
   (10) **George Cann** [9]—born 27 July, 1845; died in Demesora in South America on 19 April, 1865.
   (11) **Henry Allen Cann** [9]—born 6 June, 1846; died 20 Dec. 1859.

5. **Moses Bain** [8]—born 6 March, 1807; married **Hannah Raymond** (daughter of John); Moses died 16 Jan. 1876. *In the 1838 census, Moses' profession was listed as a tanner and there were 4 people in the household.* Moses and Hannah had 6 children:
   (1) **James Bain** [9]—died in the West Indies, 30 June, 1857.
   (2) **Rebecca Bain** [9].
   (3) **Charlotte (Bain) Raymond** [9]—married **Jachariah Raymond** of Norway, Maine.
   (4) **Wellesley Bain** [9]—born 1841; married **Sophia Cann** (daughter of Elder Calvin) on 10 June, 1866; Wellesley died 19 September, 1907. Wellesley and Sophia had 6 children:
      (i) **Bessie Bain** [10]—died young
      (ii) **Pauline Bain** [10]

      (iii) **William Bain**[10]
      (iv) **Charlotte Bain**[10]
      (v) **Bessie Bain**[10]
      (vi) **Carl Bain**[10]
  (5) **Susan Bain**[9]
  (6) **Moses Bain**[9]—married **Eliza _?** of Lynn, Mass; and they had a son named:
    (i) **Wellesley Bain**[10].

6. **Havileth (Bain) Williams**[8]—born 16 Oct. 1809, married **Benjamin Williams** (son of William). Havileth and Benjamin had 3 children:
  (1) **George Williams**[9]—born 1833; died 19 September,1859.
  (2) **William Alexander Williams**[9]—born 1836; died 7 Nov. 1845.
  (3) **Charles D. Williams**[9]—born 1843; died 12 Sept. 1865; unmarried.

7. **Mary B. (Bain) Stanwood, Goudey**[8]—married 1st **Capt. Enoch Stanwood** (son of Capt. Samuel) on 26 June,1843; 2nd **Stephen B. Goudey.** Mary died 22 February, 1890. Mary had 7 children—5 by Enoch and 2 by Stephen:

(Enoch's)
  (1) **Samuel F. Stanwood**[9]—born 13 October,1844; married **Annie R. Churchill** (daughter of Stephen) on 25 Feb. 1868.
  (2) **Effie P. Stanwood**[9]—born 21 Sept.1846; died at 2 months
  (3) **Charles Tooker Stanwood**[9]—born 23 December,1852; died at sea 1871; unmarried.
  (4) **George W. Stanwood**[9]—born 1855; died 9 Dec.1859.
  (5) **Ada Stanwood**[9]—born 19 August,1857.

(Stephen's)
  ((6) **Myra Goudey**[9]
  (7) **Grace Goudey**[9]

8. **Alice (Bain) Goudey**[8]—married **Ansel Goudey** (son of George). Alice and Ansel had 9 children:
  (1) **George Russell Goudey**[9]—born 5 January, 1838; married **Alice Rodney** (daughter of Capt. Jonathan) on 1 Nov.1862.
  (2) **Henry Goudey**[9]—born July, 1839; married **Jane Hobkirk.**
  (3) **Joseph and William** (twins) **Goudey**[9]— born 3 January, 1843; both died young.
  (4) **John Goudey**[9]—born 1844; died at sea.
  (5) **Maurice Goudey**[9]—born Dec.1846; married and lived in England .
  (6) **Robert Azor Goudey**[9]—born 24 April,1849.
  (7) **Alice (Goudey) Durkee**[9]—born 1850; married **Capt. James Durkee** (son of John).
  (8) **Jachariah Goudey**[9]—born 25 October,1851; married **Julia A. Durkee** (daughter of John).

9. <u>**James Brown Bain**</u>[8]—married 1st **Althea Porter** (daughter of Benjamin) on 13 January, 1835; 2nd **Sarah (Cann) Dalton** (widow of Calvin) on 31 January, 1857.(see page 24)

ALEXANDER BAIN III[8]

son of : Captain Alexander Bain[7], Sarah[6], Moses[5], Samuel[4], Ezra[3], Ezra[2], Edmund[1]

BORN: 14 September, 1800

MARRIED: 1st **Martha Rose** (daughter of David) on 1 January, 1825;
2nd **Edith Harris (**daughter of William) on 20 February, 1834; and 3rd
Jane Jenkins (daughter of John) on 13 November, 1836. Jane died 21
June, 1881

CHILDREN: 1. **Bethia (Bain) Allen**[9]—born 27 October, 1825; married **Joel Allen**
(by Martha Rose)   (son of Joel) on 20 December, 1867.

        2. **Martha (Bain) Porter**[9]—born 10 May, 1827; married **Benjamin Porter** (son of Hasadiah) on 30 January, 1849. Martha and Benjamin had 8 children:

           (1) **David Alexander Porter**[10]—born 4 December, 1849 ; married **Harriet Montague** (daughter of Henry) in 1870.

           (2) **Azor Dalton Porter**[10]—born 2 June, 1852; married **June Amanda Jane Hamilton** (daughter of Daniel) on 14 April, 1877.

           (3) **Martha Jane (Porter) Cushing**[10]—born 23 May, 1855; married **Capt. George Cushing** (son of George) on 2 February, 1878.

           (4) **Almira G. (Porter) Bain**[10]—born 3 June, 1857; married **William Bain** (son of Israel L.) (*see page 37*) on 15 December, 1887. They had 3 children:

             a) **Stephen Bain**[11] –born 23 February, 1889; died 17 Feb. 1890.

             b) **Lloyd Nathan Bain**[11] –born 24 September 1891, married **Gertrude Moore** and they had **Merle**[12] and **Doris Bain**[12].

             c) **Stephen Perry Bain**[11]-born 30 October 1893; married **Effie**?

           (5) **Stephen Goudey Porter**[10]—born 27 April, 1859; married **Grace Bell** (daughter of Jacob) on 15 December, 1887.

           (6) **Harriet Edna (Porter) Bain**[10]-born 7 Oct. 1860; married <u>Robert A. Bain</u> (*see page 38*)

           (7) **Benjamin F. Porter**[10]—born 1862; died 1862.

           (8) **Attilla Porter**[10]—born 1864; died 1864.

        3. **Harriet Bain**[9]—born 26 August, 1828.

        4. **Almira (Bain) Goudey**[9]—born 25 August, 1830; married **Stephen B. Goudey** (son of George) on 12 January, 1854. Almira died 14 October, 1862. Stephen married a second time **Mary B. (Bain) (Stanwood) Goudey**[8] (daughter of Alexander Bain) (widow of Capt. Enoch) who died 1 December, 1859). (*see page 26*)

        5. **Attila Bain**[9]—born 16 April, 1832; died 23 August, 1833.

(Jane Jenkin's)   6. **Alexander Bain**[9] —born 3 December, 1837; died 3 January, 1902.

        7. **John J. Bain**[9]—born 28 October, 1838; married **Caroline C. Churchill** (daughter of Jaccehaus) on 14 July, 1861. John died in the West Indies on 16 October, 1879.

        8. **David R. Bain**[9]—born 26 December, 1839; married **Mary J. Suttie** (daughter of Andrew) on 19 May, 1863. David died in Cuba on 11 Feb. 1868.

27

9. **Joseph Bain**[9]—born 2 June,1843; died 15 December,1898. Joseph married **Mary Keenan** (daughter of Terrence) on 28 August,1873 and they had 3 children:
   (1) **Ethyle M. Bain**[10]
   (2) **Blanche Bain**[10]—died 29 May, 1896; unmarried.
   (3) **Joseph Bain**[10]—killed in World War I.
10. **Sarah J. (Bain) MacGregor**[9]—born 27 June,1847; married **Norman C. MacGregor** on 12 November,1894.
11. **Sophia Bain**[9]—born 14 December,1853; died 9 January, 1869.

JAMES BROWN BAIN[8]
son of : Capt. Alexander Bain[7], Sarah[6], Moses[5], Samuel[4], Ezra[3], Ezra[2], Edmund[1]

BORN: 23 July, 1811
MARRIED: 1st **Althea Porter** (daughter of Benjamin) on 13 Jan. 1835. 2nd **Sarah (Cann) Dalton** (widow of Calvin) (*see page 24*) 31 Jan. 1857.
CHILDREN: 1. **James W. Bain**[9]—born 4 March, 1837; died 7 March,1838.
(by Althea) 2. **Mary A. (Bain) Rose**[9]—born 30 May,1839; married **George W. Rose** (son of David) on 19 December,1860. Mary and George had four children:
   (1) **Henry Rose**[10]—married **Esther Foote** (daughter of Isaac). Henry died October, 1897.
   (2) **David Rose**[10]—married **Bessie MacConnell** (daughter of Edward).
   (3) **Lois Rose**[10]—never married.
   (4) **Laura (Rose) Foote**[10]—married **Roy A. Foote** (son of James).
    3. **Harriet E. (Bain) Lovitt**[9]—born 12 February,1845; married **Capt. Thomas Lovitt** (son of Capt. Israel) (*see page 22*) on 2 March, 1867; Harriet died 10 November, 1893.
    4. **Havilla Bain**[9]—born 29 June,1849; died 29 March,1852.
(by Sarah) 5. **Althea (Bain) Corning**[9]—born 14 September,1859; married **Adolphus Corning** (son of Nelson) on 14 February,1876. Althea died November 1899 (*Pitman papers*) and is buried in the Chegoggin Cemetery. Althea and Adolphus had 8 children:
   (1) **Robert S. Corning**[10]—born 19 July, 1877.
   (2) **Murray G. Corning**[10]—born 4 July, 1879; married **Rose**.
   (3) **Ida B. (Corning) Robbins**[10]—born 20 October,1881; married **Mr.Robbins**.
   (4) **Infanta Corning**[10]—born and died on 20 May, 1883.
   (5) **Hermie Corning**[10]—born 8 September,1885; died 6 Nov. 1885.
   (6) **Frank Corning**[10]—born 14 September,1886.
   (7) **Augusta A. (Corning) (Gray) Blakeney**[10]—born 19 July, 1891; married 1st **Stanley Gray** (son of Ezra), 2nd **Edward Blakeney**.
   (8) **Jennie L. (Corning) Brown**[10]—born 10 February,1896; married **Burnett Brown** (son of George C.)
    6. **James M. Bain**[9]—born 29 November,1860; married 1st **Bessie M. Trask** (daughter of George R.) on 10 March, 1886; 2nd **Mattie**

Goodwin (widow). James died 12 December,1933. They had 9 children:
- (1) **Elsie Bain**[10]—born 27 August,1888; died 4 October, 1908.
- (2) **Percy Bain**[10]—born 2 October,1890; died 13 August, 1891.
- (3) **G. Clayton Bain**[10]—born 25 December,1891; married **Lena Foote** (daughter of Edison). G. Clayton and Lena had 2 children:
  - (i) <u>Hubert Bain</u>[11]—born 6 January,1916; married **Mildred Allen** (daughter of Fred) .
  - (ii) **Elizabeth Barbara Bain**[11]—born 14 April, 1919.
- (4) **Harry K. Bain**[10]—born 18 September,1893; married **Kitty Whiddon** of England. Harry and Kitty had three children:
  - (i) **Donald Bain**[11]—married **Elsie Campbell.**
  - (ii) **Thelma Bain**[11]
  - (iii) **Joan Bain**[11]
- (5) **Georgia Bain**[10]—born 25 March,1895; died 9 May,1897.
- (6) **Nellie (Bain) Spicer**[10]—2 October,1896; married **Roland Spicer.**
- (7) **Margaret (Bain) Trask**[10]—married **Alfred Trask** (son of Frank). They had :
  - (i) **Stuart Trask**[11]-born 23 March,1925
  - (ii) **Beverly Trask**[11]-born 5 November, 1928.
- (8) **Egbert Bain**[10]—born 1904; died in 1908.
- (9) **Mildred Bain**[10]—died in 1907 at age 9 months
7. **George Bain**[9]—born 27 May, 1863; died 24 July, 1863.
8. **Jennie (Bain) Edmund**[9]—born 24 April,1865; married **Frederick N. Edmund** from the U.S.A.
9. **Frederick Bain**[9] —born 16 March,1868.
10. **Charles Bain**[9]—born 6 February,1870; married **Agnes Gaines** of P.E.I. on 4 September, 1893. Charles and Agnes had two children:
- (1) **Sarah Agnes (Bain) Palmer**[10]—born 24 April, 1894; married **Wilbur Palmer.** Sarah and Wilbur had two children:
  - (i) **Thelma (Palmer) Fletcher**[11]—married **Albert Fletcher.**
  - (ii) **Edward Palmer**[11].
- (2) **Charles Somner Bain**[10]—born 24 April,1897; married **Freda Palmer.** Charles and Freda had one child:
  - (i) **Marie (Bain) Niacock**[11]—married Mr. **Niacock.**
11. **Sarah (Bain) Corning**[9]—born 27 March, 1872; married **John C. Corning** (son of Jefferson) on 9 March, 1893.
12. **Ida Bain**[9]—born 19 August,1874; died 6 February, 1880.
13. **Alexander Bain** [9]—born 18 November,1878; married **Jane Harris** (daughter of Reuben) on 18 May, 1900.
14. **Thomas Bain**[9]—born 16 August,1882.

HUBERT BAIN[11]

son of: G. Clayton Bain[10], James M. Bain[9], Joseph B. Bain[8], Capt. Alexander Bain [7], Sarah[6], Moses[5], Samuel[4], Ezra[3], Ezra[2], Edmund[1]

BORN: 6 January, 1916.
MARRIED: **Mildred Allen** (daughter of Fred)

CHILDREN: 1. **Doreen (Bain) McCallum**[12] —married **Douglas McCallum** (on 24 June, 1962) Doreen and Douglas had three children:
    (1) **William James McCallum**[13]
    (2) **Stewart Alan McCallum**[13].
    (3) **Sheila Dawn McCallum**[13].
  2. **James Bain**[12].

DESCENDENTS OF JOHN E. BAIN
4th child of Sarah

JOHN BAIN II[8]
son of: John E. Bain[7], Sarah[6], Moses[5], Samuel[4], Ezra[3], Ezra[2], Edmund[1]

BORN: 26 August,1804.
MARRIED: **Matilda Flint** (daughter of Capt. David).
CHILDREN: 1. **John S. Bain** [9] —born 1830; died 29 Dec. 1858; married **Emma Phillips** (daughter of Jacob K.). They had:
    (1) **Emma B. (Bain) Crosby**[10], who married **Knowles Eugene Crosby** (son of Knowles Sr.) on 1 July, 1892.
  2. **Samuel Bain**[9]—born in 1831; died 7 August,1848.
  3. **Helen (Bain) Trefry**[9]—born in 1834; married **Capt. William E. Trefry** (son of William) on 2 August,1854. Helen died 8 Oct,1864.
  4. **Martha (Bain) Weldon**[9]—born 1837; married **Charles Weldon** (Wilmont, N.S.) on 2 April,1854. Martha died 5 December,1864.
  5. **Mary Elizabeth (Bain) Raymond**[9]—born 1842; married **Jack A. Raymond** (Norway, Maine) on 12 Nov. 1859. Mary Elizabeth died on 1 December,1860.
  6. **Matilda Bain**[9]—born in 1858; died 15 December,1859.

DESCENDENTS OF SAMUEL BAIN
6th child of Sarah

SAMUEL BAIN[7]
son of: Sarah[6], Moses[5], Samuel[4], Ezra[3], Ezra[2], Edmund[1]

BORN: 14 November,1785
MARRIED: 1st **Eunice Landers** (daughter of Jabez); 2nd **Hannah Kelley** (daughter of Capt. James).
DIED: 14 September,1850.
CHILDREN: 1. **Deborah (Bain) Redding**[8]—married **Herbert Redding** (son of Benjamin).
  2. **Samuel Thorndyke Bain**[8]—born 1812; married 1st **Mary Porter** (daughter of Hasadiah); 2nd **Almira (Goudey) Churchill** (widow of John). Samuel died 22 April, 1888.
  3. **Lois (Bain) DeWolfe**[8]—married **Capt. Charles DeWolfe** son of Simon) on 7 February, 1855.
  4. **Alexander Bain**[8]—born 1815; married **Alice Baker** (daughter of Jonathan) Alexander and Alice had 9 children:

(1) **Amelia Bain**[9] —died young.

(2) **Alexander Bain**[9]—born 1840; died 1902; married **Sarah Crosby Patten** (daughter of Stephen). Alexander and Sarah had 3 children:

  (i) **Clara E. (Bain) Redding**[10]—born 1870, died 1943; married **Edward Redding** (son of W.H.).

  (ii) **Alva (Bain) Perry**[10]—married **Gordon Perry** (son of Miner). Gordon died in Nov. 1949. Alva and Gordon had 4 children:

    a) **Graham Perry** [11]

    b) **Gordon Perry**[11]

    c) **Doreen Perry**[11]

    d) **Carol Perry**[11].

  (iii) **Murray S. Bain**[10].

(3) _____**Bain**[9]—died 9 March, 1903.

(4) **James Bain**[9]—born in 1844; married **Cynthia Trask** (daughter of James) on 18 December,1879. James died 8 February,1911. James and Cynthia had 3 children:

  (i) **Fanny Bain**[10]—born 1881; died 8 December, 1898.

  (ii) **George Bain**[10].

  (iii) **Harry Bain**[10]—died aged 3 months.

(5) **George Bain**[9]—died unmarried.

(6) **Maria (Bain) Powers**[9]—married **Nathaniel Powers** (son of James).

(7) **Jacob Bain**[9]—died unmarried.

(8) **Alva Bain**[9]—died unmarried.

(9) **Sophia Bain**[9]—born 1819, died 1875; never married.

5. **Eunice (Bain) Durkee**[8]—married **William E. Durkee** (son of Robert).

6. **William Bain**[8]—born in 1818; married 1st **Lydia Ann Patten** (daughter of John) Lydia died 30 November, 1880, 2nd **Mary (Patten) Raymond**, (widow of Benjamin); William died 13 March,1897. They had 12 children:

(1) **George William Bain**[9]—born 1839; married **Fanny Raymond** (daughter of Ira).

(2) **Nathaniel Patten Bain**[9]—born 10 September,1839; married **Laura (Robbins) Bain** (widow of brother John).

(3) **Samuel A . Bain**[9]—born 15 August,1843; married 1st **Hannah Richardson** (daughter of Samuel) on 2 August, 1873 *(see page 66)* 2nd**Labitta Richardson** (daughter of Samuel). Labitta died in 1921 at age 75. Samuel died in 1937.

(4) **Maria Ellen (Bain) Clements**[9]—born 14 September,1845 in Yarmouth; (*Clements' Genealogy states she was born 13 Nov. 1847).* She married **Edwin Clements** (son of Capt. Charles).Edwin was born 1845 and died in 1921. Maria died 8 December,1838 in Danvers, Massachusetts. They had a son:

  (i) **Joseph B. Clements**[10]- born 1879 and died in 1909. He is buried in Riverside Cemetery, Yarmouth.

(5) **Joseph Patten Bain**[9]—born 1 November,1847; married **Sarah Odessa Crosby** (daughter of Joseph H.). Joseph died 17 August,1894.

(6) **John Perry Bain**[9]—born 30 August,1849; married **Laura Robbins**. John was lost at sea 24 November,1875. Laura later married **Nathaniel Bain** [9](brother of John).

(7) **Stephen Rose Bain**[9]—born 24 July,1851; married **Elizabeth King** (daughter of Henry).

(8) **Benjamin Raymond Bain**[9]—born 29 March,1853; married **Laliah Perry** (daughter of Stephen).(see page 64)
They had a son:
  (i) **Benjamin R. Bain** [10]—married **Alice Trask** on 23 July, 1914. Benjamin and Alice had 3 children:
    a). **Allister Bain**[11].
    b). **Raymond Bain**[11].
    c). **Rita Mae Bain**[11].

(9) **Enos Patten Bain**[9]—born 16 August,1854; married **Augusta Walsh** of Portland, Maine.

(10) **Norman Bain**[9]—born 8 April,1857; married **Caroline Riordan**.

(11) **Lois S. (Bain) Durkee**[9]—born 17 April,1859; married **Jesse Durkee** (son of Samuel).

(12) **Augustus Rose Bain**[9]—born 30 March,1862; married 1st **Jessie M. Pearl** on 1 June 1892; 2nd **Blanche Ethel Durkee** on 22 Sept. 1909. Augustus died 1911. Augustus Rose and Jessie had at least one child:
  (i) **Muriel (Bain) Kedder**[10] —married **Mr. Kedder** (widower of Medfod).

7. **Sophia Killiam (Bain) Steele**[8]—married **John Steele** on 21 Nov.1840.

SAMUEL THORNDYKE BAIN[8]

son of: Samuel Bain[7] , Sarah[6], Moses[5], Samuel[4], Ezra[3], Ezra[2], Edmund[1].

MARRIED: 1st **Mary Porter** (daughter of Hasadiah), 2nd **Almira (Goudey) Churchill** (widow of John).

DIED: 22 April, 1888.

CHILDREN: 1. **Eunice (Bain) Pitman**[9]—married **David Pitman** (son of Asa) on 10 November,1853.

2. **Asa Bain**[9]—married **Harriet Cynthia Rodney** (daughter of Samuel) on 30 October, 1857.

3. **Mary Anne (Bain) Foote**[9]—married **Norman Foote** (son of Jachariah).

4. **William Bain**[9]—moved to Fredericton, New Brunswick.

5. **Margaret E. (Bain) Patten**[9]—married **Benjamin P. Patten** (son of William S.) on 24 December,1856.

6. **Emily Hannah (Bain) Crosby**[9]—married **Thomas P. Crosby** (son of Reuben).

7. **Hasadiah Bain**[9]—moved to the United States.

8. **Edward Edgar Bain**[9]— married **Amelia Harris** (daughter of George & Priscilla (Bain) Harris from Pembroke, Nova Scotia) in 1854. (see page 34). Edgar and Amelia had 2 children:
  (1) **Richard Bain**[10]—married **Vivian Lyons** (daughter of Charles from Chegoggin, Nova Scotia).Richard and Vivian had 2 children:
    (i) **Frances Bain**[11]

(ii) **Edgar Bain**[11].
(2) **Mary Bain**[10].

DESCENDENTS OF WILLIAM BAIN
7th child of Sarah

WILLIAM BAIN[7]
son of: Sarah[6], Moses[5], Samuel[4], Ezra[3], Ezra[2], Edmund[1]

BORN: 10 April, 1787
MARRIED: **Asenath Porter** (daughter of Hasadiah).
CHILDREN: 1. **William Bain**[8]—married **Margaret Cook** (daughter of
Manassah II). Margaret was born in 1828 and died in 1912.
William died in 1915. William and Margaret had 8 children:

(1) **Asenath (Bain) (Vickery) Allen** [9] (twin of Delancey) —born 20
Feb. 1857. Asenath married 1st **Benjamin Vickery** (son of Samuel
of Deerfield) and 2nd married **George Israel Allen** (son of James of
Ohio, Nova Scotia) on 15 April ,1882. Asenath died 7 September,
1947.

(2) **Delancey Bain**[9] (twin of Asenath)—born 20 Feb. 1857. Delancey
married **Augusta Bell** (daughter of Capt. Robert) and they had 9
children. Delancey died in May of 1946 in Walla Walla, Washington.

*It is often reported that Conrad Bain, the actor who played the
father, Phillip Drummond, in the late 1970's TV Series
"Different Strokes" was the grandson of Delancey. Conrad
was Canadian (Alberta), and was a twin (Bonar), but his
father was Stafford Harrison Bain, son of Grant Ulysses Bain.
I can find no link to Delancey!*

(i) <u>**Robert Bain**</u>[10]—married **Eva Hilton**
(ii) **Arthur Bain**[10]
(iii) **Elmer Bain**[10]
(iv) **Lizzie (Bain) Hurlburt**[10]—married **Melford Hurlburt** (son
of John).
(v) **Margaret Bain**[10]
(vi) **Garfield Bain**[10]
(vii) **Ada Bain**[10]
(viii) **Hilda Bain**[10]
(ix) **Fredrick Bain**[10]

(3) **Sarah A. (Bain) Scoville**[9]—married **Reuben Scoville** (son of
James R.) on 24 May, 1876.

(4) **Annis (Bain) Bell**[9]—married **Edward Bell** (son of Robert)

(5) **Laura (Bain) Harris**[9]—born in 1861; married **Reuben Harris** (son
of Edward). Laura died 4 September, 1901.

(6) <u>**George Bain**</u>[9]— born in 1862; married **Alice Foote**
(daughter of Norman). George died in 1944.

(7) **Sophia (Bain) Smith**[9]—married **Joseph Smith** (son of Elias).

(8) **Emma (Bain) Rose**[9]—married **William B. Rose** (son of Jacob K.) on 22 December, 1888.

2. **Hasadiah Bain**[8]—married **Hannah Foot** (daughter of Capt.Robert). Hasadiah and Hannah 2 children:

(1) **John William Bain**[9]—born 1852; married **Mary Ellen Cann** (daughter of James C.). John died in 1927. John and Mary had:

(i) **Mary (Bain) Allen**[10] who married **Gilbert J. Allen** (son of George Israel).

(2) **Robert Bain**[9]—married 1st **Lois Landers** (daughter of Herman), and 2nd **Marion (Cook) Porter** (widow of Jacob). Robert and Lois had:

(i) **Bradford Bain** [10]-married **Hilda Allen** (daughter of George Israel).

(ii) **Herman Bain**[10]

(iii) **Frances Bain**[10] who died young.

3. **Israel L. Bain**[8]—married **Jane Scoville** (daughter of Nathan) on 27 January,1853.

4. **Priscilla (Bain) Harris**[8]—married **George Harris** (son of Ebenezer). Priscilla and George had 5 children:

(1) **Judson J. Harris**[9]— married **Annie Worthline** (daughter of Moses) in 1881.

(2) **George Harris**[9]

(3) **Amelia (Harris) Bain**[9]—married **Edward "Edgar" Bain** (son of Samuel Thorndyke*).(see page 32)*

(4) **Hannah (Harris) Rogers**[9]—married **Thomas Rogers**.

(5) **Priscilla Harris**[9].

Israel L. Bain

ROBERT BAIN[10]

son of: Delancey Bain[9], William Bain[8], William Bain[7], Sarah[6], Moses[5], Samuel[4], Ezra[3], Ezra[2], Edmund[1]

MARRIED: **Eva Hilton** (daughter of Jeremiah).

CHILDREN: 1. **Iva (Bain) Chambers**[11]—married **William Chambers**.

2. **Jeremiah Bain**[11]—married **Louise Andrews**.

3. **Ada (Bain) Geddrie**[11]—married **Melvin Geddrie**.

4. **Robert Bain**[11]—married **Helen Thibodeau** (daughter of James) . Robert and Helen had 7 children:

(1) **Iva and Jeremiah** (twins) **Bain**[12]— both died in infancy.

(2) **James Bain**[12].

(3) **Henry Bain**[12]—drowned in a well in 1946 at age 2.

(4) **George Bain**[12]

(5) **Hubert Bain**[12]

(6) **Helen Bain**[12]

5. **Eva Bain**[11]—died at age 3.

GEORGE BAIN[9]

son of: William Bain[8], William Bain[7], Sarah[6], Moses[5], Samuel[4], Ezra[3], Ezra[2], Edmund[1]

BORN: 1862.
DIED: 1944.
MARRIED: **Alice Foote** (daughter of Norman).
CHILDREN: 1. **Irvin Bain**[10]—married 1st **Alice**, 2nd **?** —,3rd **Edith**.
           2. **Leslie G. Bain**[10]—married **Lulu Brannen** on 21 Jan. 1909.
             Leslie and Lulu had 6 children:
             (1) **Gerald Bain**[11]—married **Edith Cushing** (daughter of
                Edward). They had a daughter:
                (i) **Beatrice Bain**[12]-born in 1940; died 28 April, 2008. "Beatti" was a
                    banker and a bookkeeper.
             (2) **Carl Bain**[11]—married **Hope Ros**e (daughter of Arley). They
                had two children:
                (i) **Irva Bain**[12]
                (ii) **lan Bain** [12]
             (3) <u>**Burnley Bain**</u>[11] —married **Alva Scoville** (daughter of
                Herbert). Burnley and Alva had two children.
             (4) **George St. Clare Bain**[11]—married 1st **Catherine Olson**
                (daughter of William) and they had:
                (i) **Larry Bain**[12].
           George and Catherine divorced and he married 2nd **Margaret_?**
    George married 3rd **Anna (Doucette) Fitzgerald** and they had one child:
                (ii) **Michael Bain**[12].
             (5) **Douglas Bain**[11]—1st married **Jane Boudreau.** They were
                divorced and Douglas married 2nd **Mineva Doucette.**
             (6) **Joyce (Bain) (Lamb)Brizet**[11]—married 1st **Anthony Lamb** of
                England. Joyce and Anthony had:
              (i) **Alice Dale Lamb**[12]—born 14 October,1946; died 2 days later.
                Joyce married 2nd **Maurice Brizet.** Joyce and Maurice had three
                children:
              (ii) **Kenney Brizet**[12]
               (iii) **Marty Brizet**[12]
               (iv) **Shelley Brizet**[12].
           Joyce and Maurice now have 6 grandchildren.
           3. **Margaret (Bain) Trask**[10]—married **Arnold Trask** (son of Charles)
             on 2 November,1903. Margaret and Arnold had 8 children:
             (1) one drowned.
             (2) **Walter Trask**[11]—married **Hope Baker** (daughter of Lloyd).
             (3) **Eva Trask**[11]
             (4) **Irvin Trask**[11]—married **Jennie Williams** (adopted
                daughter of Charles).
             (5) **Phyllis Trask**[11]
             (6) **Lila Trask**[11]
             (7) **Pearl (Trask) Stewart**[11]—married **David Stewart**
             (8) **Muriel Trask**[11].

4. **Catherine (Bain) Shaw**[10]—married **James Zebina Shaw**.
   Catherine and James had 3 children:
   (1) **Murray Shaw**[11]
   (2) **Eva Shaw**[11]
   (3) **Irvan Shaw**[11]
5. **Dean Bain**[10]—married **Nellie Crosby** (daughter of Ebenezer and
   Matilda (Huskins) Crosby) on 9 March, 1915. Dean and Nellie had 4
   children:
   (1) **Eugene Bain**[11]—married **Faye Scoville.** Eugene and Faye had
       2 children:
       (i) **Richard Bain**[12]
       (ii) **Cheryl Bain**[12]
   (2) **Kathleen (Bain) Gray**[11]—married **Marshall Gray** (son of
       Stanley and Augusta " Greta" Gray).(See page 28)
   (3) **Forrester Bain**[11]—married **Muriel Moses** (daughter of Glindon).
   (4) **Phyllis (Bain) Fuller**[11]—married **Carl Fuller** (son of Albert and
       Edith (Pitman)Fuller).
6. **Addie (Bain) Porter**[10]—married **Charles Porter** (son of Samuel)
   Addie and Charles had 3 children:
   (1) **Spencer Porter**[11]—died
   (2) **Rayden Porter**[11]—by adoption.
   (3) **Malcolm Porter**[11].
7. **Nellie (Bain) Cann**[10]—married **Charles Loran Cann** (son of
   Staley).
8. **Willis Bain**[10]—married **Marion Crosby** (daughter of George)
9. **Bertley Bain**[10]—married **Susan Cook** (daughter of Howard S.)
10. **Raymond Bain**[10]—married **Theora Randall** (daughter of Dexter
    and Maggie (Ring) Randall).
    (1) **Evelyn Bain**[11].
    (2) **Audrey Bain**[11].
11. **George Bain**[10]—married **Jean?** of Toronto. They had:
    (1) **Keith Bain** [11]
12. **Frances Bain**[10]—died in infancy.
13. **Roy Bain**[10]—married **Mabel Gray** (daughter of Edgar). Roy and
    Mabel had 3 children:
    (1) **Burton Bain**[11].
    (2) **Harold Bain**[11]
    (3) **Jean Bain**[11]
14. **Clarence Bain**[10]—married **Reta Archer** (daughter of Fred and
    Clara (Wyman) Archer). They had a daughter:
    (1) **Gloria Bain**[11].
15. **Edgar Bain**[10]—married **Hilda Hayward**.

BURNLEY BAIN[11]
son of: Leslie G. Bain[10], George Bain[9], William Bain[8], William Bain[7],
Sarah[6], Moses[5], Samuel[4], Ezra[3], Ezra[2], Edmund[1]

MARRIED: **Alva Margaret Scoville** (1917-2013)(daughter of Herbert).
CHILDREN: 1. **Roger Bain**[12]—married **Sharon Limber** (from Alberta). Roger and
Sharon had two children:
(1) **Tracy LaRae Bain**[13]
(2) **Bradley Roger Bain**[13]
2. **Ronald St Clair Bain**[12]—married **Louise Milbury** (daughter of Alena
and Harry). Ronald and Louise had:
(1). **Peter David St. Clair Bain**[13]
(2). **Elizabeth Louise Bain**[13]
*information on the Leslie G. Bain Family and the Burnley Bain Family courtesy of Alva
Scoville Bain*

BRADFORD BAIN[10]
son of: Robert Bain[9], Hasadiah Bain[8], William Bain [7], Sarah[6], Moses[5],
Samuel[4], Ezra[3], Ezra[2], Edmund[1]
Was police chief of Yarmouth, Nova Scotia for many years
MARRIED **Hilda Allen** (daughter of George Israel).
CHILDREN: 1. **Clayton Bain**[11].
2. **Lillian (Bain) Jeffery**[11]—married **Frank Jeffery** (son of Frank).
They had a son:
(1) **James Jeffery**[12].
3. **Bradford Bain**[11]—married **Alice Crosby** (daughter of Leslie). They
had a daughter:
(1) **Barbara Ann Bain**[12].
4. **Robert Israel Bain**[11].(1927-2013**)**. Married **Beulah** and had **Kim**[12],
Dawn[12], **Kandy**[12], **Kent**[12] and **Robin**[12]
5. **Lois Bain**[11].

ISRAEL L. BAIN[8]
son of: William Bain[7] , Sarah[6], Moses[5], Samuel[4], Ezra[3], Ezra[2], Edmund[1]

MARRIED: **Alice Jane Scoville** (daughter of Nathan) on 27 January, 1853.
CHILDREN: 1. <u>**Melitta Jane (Bain) Clements**</u>[9]—born 24 November, 1853; married
George Clements (son of George of Westport, Nova Scotia).
2. **Amanda (Bain) Pugh**[9]—married **John Pugh**.
3. <u>Israel Bain </u>[9]—married 1st ?**King** (daughter of Robert from Arcadia);
2nd **Martha (or Matilda) Denton.**
4. **William Bain**[9]—married **Almira G. Porter** : *(see page 27)* (daughter
of Benjamin, the son of Hasadiah) on 15 December, 1887. William
and Almira had 3 children
(1) **Stephen Bain**[10]—born 23 Feb. 1889; died 17 Feb. 1890.
(2) **Lloyd Nathan Bain**[10]—born 24 September, 1891; married
Gertrude Moore. Lloyd Nathan and Gertrude had 2 children;
(i) **Merle Bain**[11].
(ii) **Doris Bain**[11].

(3) **Stephen Perry Bain**[10]—born 30 October,1893; married **Effie?**—

5. **Robert A. Bain**[9]— born 1863; married **Harriet Edna Porter** (born 1861) (daughter of Benjamin of Hasadiah) on 23 March, 1888. *(see page 27)* Robert died 1918. Harriet died 1935. Robert and Harriet had 5 children:
   (1) **Kenneth Ross Bain**[10]— born 5 April, 1889.
   (2) **Jenson Carl Bain**[10]—born 15 May, 1890.
   (3) **Fanny P.** and **Frances** (twins) **Bain**[10]. Fanny married **Whitman Killiam** (son of Isaac) and Frances married **Earle Allen** (son of Israel L.) on 23 October, 1913.
   (4) **Cora Lee Bain**[10]—born 8 August, 1893.

6. **Harriet (Bain) Foote**[9]—married **Lockhart Foote** (son of Norman)

7. Nathan **Bain**[9]—born 1870; married **Ina King** (daughter of Robert) Nathan died 1935.

8. **Howard Bain**[9]—married **Margaret Larkin.**

9. **Percy Bain**[9] —married **Lottie Foote** and they had three children:
   (1) **Erma Bain**[10]—died in 1989, never married.
   (2) **Blake Bain**[10]—died in infancy in 1901.
   (3) **Barbara (Bain) Arms**[10]—born in 1917, she died 11 Feb. 2006. She married **Harry F. Arms.** They had:
     (i) **Carol (Arms) Allen**[11]—married **Samuel Allen** and they had two children:
       a). **John Allen**[12]
       b). **Donna Allen**[12]
     (ii) **Wayne Arms**[11]—married **Roberta?** and they had one child:
       a) **Craig Arms**[12]
     (iii) **Joan (Arms) Nelson**[11]—married **Robert Nelson.** No children.

10. **Ainsley L. Bain**[9]—born in 1876, married **Maude Wilkes** from Ontario on 5 May, 1907. Ainsley and Maude had 3 sons: **Harold**[10], **Truman**[10] and **Chester Bain**[10]

11. **James E. Bain**[9]—married **Ida Denton.** James was a carpenter. He and Ida had 2 sons:
   (1) **Vincent Bain**[10]—married 1st **Edna Pierce**, 2nd **Reta_?**
   (2) **Reginald Bain** [10]—married **Annie** in the United States.

MELITTA JANE (BAIN) CLEMENTS[9]
daughter of: Israel L. Bain[8], William Bain [7], Sarah[6], Moses[5], Samuel[4], Ezra[3], Ezra[2], Edmund[1]

BORN: 24 November, 1853
MARRIED: **George William Clements** (son of William Elkanah from Westport). George William was born on the 25th of March, 1852 at sea off the coast of Scotland and died in February of 1929 in Westport, Nova Scotia.
DIED: 24 October, 1925.

CHILDREN: 1. **Mabel S. Clements**[10]—born in 1874 and died 26 April, 1897; drowned in Halifax Harbour and was buried at Pembroke Shore.

From the *Halifax Tri-Weekly*, page 2, April 27, 1897
A Girl Disappears
Halifax was startled yesterday morning to hear what appears much like a suicide. A girl, Mabel Clements, 23 years of age, who was a general servant with Mr. Rod MacDonald, 433 Brunswick St, is the victim of the supposed tragedy.

It appears that Miss Clements had a lover Lewis Foote, who is reported to have been untrue to her. Miss Clements, in company with Mr. MacDonald's nurse girl, left home Saturday evening between 7 and 8 and called at Miss Clement's home on Barrington Street, and also at MacPherson & Freeman's. They were returning home about 9:40, when Lewis Foote met them and escorted them to Mr. MacDonald's, arriving there at or about 10 o'clock. Miss Clements told her girl chum that she would be in in a few minutes. That was the last time her chum saw her.

In the morning the entire household was alarmed at Miss Clement's absence and a search was at once instituted for her ... Lewis Foote said he left her at Mr. MacDonald's residence about 15 minutes after the nurse girl went into the house. Yesterday evening, her purse was found at the north ferry wharf.

From the **Halifax Mail** April 28, 1897

The body of Mabel Clements was found this morning at 11:45 by diver Samuel Smith.

The Mail talked to Lewis Foote, to whom the deceased was engaged. He said he walked with both girls to Mr. MacDonald's home on Brunswick Street. The cousin went into the house and left Miss Clements and Foote at the door. The girl informed Foote that every time that she went to her home, her mother quarreled with her. In the middle of the conversation, she suddenly stopped and said, "What time does the last boat leave the north ferry slip at night?" Foote said he did not know. She asked Foote to take the gold watch, which he had given her as it reminded her of her home and him every time she looked at it, it occasioned sorrow. Foote took the watch and told the girl that he would leave it with her mother, where she could obtain it at any time. He said good night, when leaving she ascended the stairs in front of MacDonald's house, and he thought went in. Mrs. Clements informed the Mail that she and her daughter were always on friendly terms. She stated that some time ago, her daughter spoke of drowning herself because of a coolness that had arisen between her and Foote. The medical examiner's report states: " Death was due to suicide by drowning while temporarily insane".

  2. **Lizzie E. Clements**[10]—born in 1875 and died in 1888 in Pembroke .
  3. **William Clements**[10]—born in 1877. William was a barber by trade. He sold his business and was going "out west". He started his journey from Digby to St. John, New Brunswick, and was never heard of again.

4. **Harvey G. Clements**[10]—born 1879 and died in 1893. Harvey died of a heart condition at a young age. He died in the Victoria General Hospital, Halifax and was buried in Pembroke Shore.

5. **Robert Kelly Clements** [10]—born 30 March, 1886 in Ohio, Nova Scotia; married **Mary Ruth Stewart** and died on 17 May, 1982.

6. **Daisy Gladys (Clements) Lockwood**[10]—born 22 September, 1895; married **Henry Cecil Lockwood** who was born 8 April, 1891 and died 5 February, 1959. Daisy Gladys died 28 May,1984. Daisy Gladys and Henry Cecil had 3 children:

   (1) **George Lockwood**[11].

   (2) **Kathleen Shirley (Lockwood) Sawler**[11]—born 20 May,1921 and married **Aubrey Alfred Sawler** who was born 20 March, 1912 and died 30 June, 1975.

   (3) **Muriel Jean (Lockwood) Killin**[11]—born 7 May, 1926; married **Raymond John Killin** who was born 17 October, 1920 and who died 7 October, 1992

ROBERT KELLY CLEMENTS[10]

son of: Melitta Jane (Bain) Clements[9], Israel L. Bain[8], William Bain[7], Sarah[6], Moses[5], Samuel[4], Ezra[3], Ezra[2], Edmund[1]

BORN: 30 March, 1886 in Ohio, Nova Scotia.

MARRIED: **Mary Ruth Stewart** on 19 April, 1916 in Kensington, Prince Edward Island. Mary Ruth was born on 15 January, 1895 on Prince Edward Island and died on 23 December, 1979, in Montague, Prince Edward Island.

DIED: 17 May, 1982 in Charlottetown, Prince Edward Island.

CHILDREN: 1. **Robert Kelly Clements**[11]—born 10 March, 1920; and married **Eileen Tomey** who was born on 12 July, 1923. Robert Kelly died 3 Oct.1943.

2. **Mary Ruth Melitta (Clements) Bell**[11]—born 5 December, 1921; married **John Robert Bell** who was born on the 5 May, 1918. Mary Ruth and John Robert had 2 children:

   (1) **Nancy Elizabeth Bell**[12].

   (2) **Mary Joanne (Bell) Mutch**[12]; married **Ernest Roy Mutch.** Mary Joanne and Ernest Roy had two children:

   (i) **Stephen John Mutch**[13].

   (ii) **Julie Anne Mutch**[13]

3. **Nellie Jean (Clements) Patterson**[11] —born 11 September,1926; married **Malcolm Grenville Patterson** who was born 9 June, 1926. Nellie Jean and Malcolm had 3 children:

   (1) **Linda Marlene (Patterson) Gibson**[12]—married **John Murray Gibson** . Linda Marlene and John Murray had two children:

   (i) **Melda Leanne Gibson**[13]

   (ii) **Geoffry Neil Gibson**[13]

   (2) **Brenda Eileen (Patterson) Burns**[12]—married **Derek Scott Burns.** Brenda Eileen and Derek Scott had one child:

   (i) **Hannah Jane Burns**[13]

   (3) **Melda Elaine (Patterson) Jones**[12]—married **Robert Lee Jones.** Melda Elaine and Robert Lee had two children:

   (i) **Mallory Elaine Jones**[13]

(ii) **Monica Anne Jones**[13]

4. **Gilbert Ralph Clements (Hon)**[11]—born 11 September, 1928; married **Wilma Catherine MacLure** who was born 10 August,1933. Gilbert and Wilma had 4 children:
  (1) **Errol Gilbert Clements**[12]—born 18 June,1954; died the same day.
  (2) **Robert Kelly Clements** [12]—married **Winnifred Carol Creed**. Robert Kelly and Winnifred Carol had three children:
    (i) **Julie Ann Clements**[13]
    (ii) **Mary Catherine Clements**[13].
    (iii) **Robert Steven Clements**[13].
  (3) **David George Clements**[12]
  (4) **Mary Gail (Clements) MacDonald**[12]—married **Brian Keith MacDonald**. Mary Gail and Brian Keith had two children:
    (i) **Meaghan Brianne MacDonald**[13]
    (ii) **Scott Andrew MacDonald**[13]

5. **Kenneth Stewart Clements** [11]—born 5 November, 1929; married **Thelma Mary Coffin** who was born 20 December,1928. Kenneth Stewart died 9 January, 1990. Kenneth and Thelma had 4 children:
  (1) **Glenda Ruth (Clements) MacDonald**[12]—married **Cyril Louis MacDonald.** Glenda Ruth and Cyril Louis had three children:
    (i) **Bobbi Michelle MacDonald**[13]
    (ii) **John Kenneth Luke MacDonald**[13]
    (iii) **Shanna Colleen MacDonald**[13]
  (2) **Janice Marion (Clements) Nicolle**[12]-married **Judson Roderick Nicolle.** Janice Marion and Judson Roderick had two children:
    (i) **Jonathan Stewart Nicolle**[13]
    (ii) **Kenneth Judson Nicolle**[13]
  (3) **John Kenneth Clements**[12]—married **Kathy Elizabeth Jean Ennis.** John Kenneth and Kathy Elizabeth Jean had three children:
    (i) **Jonah Robert Kenneth Clements**[13] (twin of Mary Janel).
    (ii) **Mary Janel Elaine Clements**[13] (twin of Jonah Robert Kenneth)
    (iii) **Kristen Elizabeth Jean Clements**[13]
  (4) **Pamela Colleen (Clements) Hume**[12]-married **Mark Phillip Hume**. Pamela Colleen and Mark Phillip had three children:
    (i) **Janice Courtney Hume**[13]
    (ii) **Lindsay Marie Hume**[13].
    (iii) **Ashlee Margaret Hume**[13]

6. **Francis Pauline Clements**[11]—born and died on 2 May,1932 .

7. **Walter Leigh Clements**[11]—born 22 Nov.1933 and died 8 April, 1934.

8. **Arthur Bain Clements**[11]—married **Dorothy Faye MacDonald** Arthur and Dorothy had 3 children:
  (1) **William Leslie Clements**[12].

(2) **Dorothy Ann (Clements) Farrell**[12]-married **Gregory A. Farrell**. Dorothy Ann and Gregory had one child:
   (i) **Gregory Chance Farrell**[13]
(3) **Brenda Arlene (Clements) Lannigan**[12]—married **Neil Lannigan**.

KATHLEEN SHIRLEY (LOCKWOOD) SAWLER[11]
daughter of: Daisy Gladys (Clements) Lockwood[10], Melitta Jane (Bain) Clements[9], Israel L. Bain[8], William Bain[7], Sarah (Perry) Bain[6], Moses[5], Samuel[4], Ezra[3], Ezra[2], Edmund[1]

BORN: 20 May, 1921
MARRIED: **Aubrey Alfred Sawler** who was born 20 March, 1912 and died 30 June, 1975.
CHILDREN: 1. **Aubrey Henry Sawler**[12]—married **Judith Lynn Swan** who was born 14 February, 1944. Aubrey and Judith had 3 children:
   (1) **Terry Lee Sawler**[13] —born 16 Feb.1962 and died the same day.
   (2) **Deborah Lynn (Sawler) Cade**[13]—married **Stephen Kelly Cade**. Deborah Lynn and Stephen Kelly had two children:
     (i) **Joshua Stephen Cade**[14]
     (ii) **Cory James Cade**[14]
   (3) **Krista Lee (Sawler) Witherspoon**[13]—married **Robert Terrence Witherspoon** .
  2. **Joan Marie (Sawler) Brumm**[12]—married **Grant William Brumm** who was born on 12 November,1943 and who died 17 August, 1986. Joan Marie and Grant William had 2 children:
   (1) **David Charles Brumm**[13]—married **Betty Jean Thompson**. David Charles and Betty Jean had two children:
     (i) **Stephen Aubrey Bruce Brumm**[14]
     (ii) **Katlyn Laura Marie Brumm**[14].
   (2). **Donald Patrick Brumm**[13]—married **Christel Lee Bright** . Donald Patrick and Christel Lee had two children:
     (i) **Kristopher Robert Grant Brumm**[14]
     (ii) **Alexander Kenneth Donald Brumm**[14]

MURIEL JEAN (LOCKWOOD) KILLIN[11]
daughter of: Daisy Gladys (Clements) Lockwood[10], Melitta Jane (Bain) Clements[9], Israel L. Bain[8], William Bain[7], Sarah (Perry) Bain[6], Moses[5], Samuel[4], Ezra[3], Ezra[2], Edmund[1]

BORN: 7 May, 1926
MARRIED: **Raymond John Killin** who was born on 17 October,1920 and who died 7 October, 1992.
CHILREN: 1. **Paula Rayden (Killin) Olsen**[12]—married **Kjeld Seidelin Olsen** Paula Rayden and Kjeld Seidelin had four children:
   (1) **Calvin Douglas Olsen**[13].
   (2) **Dean Paul Olsen**[13] -married **Michelle Lynn Buehling**. Dean Paul and Michelle Lynn had two children:
     (i) **Magon Lynelle Olsen**[14]

        (ii) **Casey James Olsen**[14]
      (3) **Lana Jean (Olsen) Bodenhamer**[13]—married **Thad Scott Bodenhamer**. Lana Jean and Thad Scott had one child:
        (i) **Cade Alan Bodenhamer**[14].
      (4) **Pamela Lee (Olsen) Gressett**[13]-married **Michael Everett Gressett**. Pamela Lee and Michael Everett had two children:
        (i) **Logan Michael Gressett**[14].
        (ii) **Blair Lee Gressett**[14].
  2. **Nancy Louise (Killin) Echlin**[12]—married **Peter Allan Echlin**. Nancy Louise and Peter Allan had two children:
    (1) **Lori Louise Echlin**[13]
    (2) **Blair Allan Echlin**[13].
  3. **Peter George Killin**[12]—married **Norma Patrice LeCain.** Peter George and Norma Patrice had three children:
    (1) **Michael Peter Killin**[13]
    (2) **Matthew Patrick Killin**[13] (twin of Robert John)
    (3) **Robert John Killin**[13] (twin of Matthew Patrick)
4. **Murray James Killin**[12]—married **Julie Teresa Brooks.** Murray James and Julie Teresa had two children:
    (1) **Jennifer Elizabeth Killin**[13]
    (2) **David James Killin**[13]

information on the Melitta Jane (Bain) Clements Family courtesy of the Hon. Gilbert Clements.

ISRAEL BAIN[9]
son of: Israel L. Bain[8], William Bain[7], Sarah[6], Moses[5], Samuel[4], Ezra[3], Ezra[2], Edmund[1]

MARRIED: 1st **Miss King** (daughter of Robert from Arcadia)
            2nd **Martha (or Matilda) Denton**

CHILDREN: 1. **Elizabeth (Bain) Churchill**[10]—married **Herman Churchill** (son of Amos).
        2. **Edna (Bain) Durkee**[10]—married **Clifford Durkee** (son of John).
        3. **Sydney Bain**[10]—married **Mabel Durkee** (daughter of Bradford). They had a son;
        (1) **Howard B. Bain**[11]—born 1924 and died in 1929.
        4. **Everett Bain**[10]—married **Miss Harris** (daughter of Norman). Everett and his wife had 6 children:
          (1) **Charles Bain**[11]—married **Goldie Stevens** (daughter of Dalton). They had a son:
            (i) **Ivan Bain**[12].
          (2) **Harry Bain**[11]—married Miss **Sears** (daughter of Rowena). They had a son:
            (i) **Charles Bain**[12].
          (3) **Clayton Bain**[11].
          (4) **Flora (Bain) Rodney**[11]—married **Hugh Rodney** (son of Evans and Martha (Churchill) Rodney) on 16 Feb. 1942.
          (5) **Stella (Bain) Lander**[11]—married **Percy Landers.**
          (6) **Adelbert Bain**[11]—married **Alice Durkee** (daughter of Reuben and Margaret (Diedritch) Durkee).They had 2 daughters:

    (i) **Margaret Bain**[12]
    (ii) **Florence Bain**[12].

NATHAN BAIN[9]
son of: Israel L. Bain[8], William Bain[7], Sarah[6], Moses[5], Samuel[4], Ezra[3], Ezra[2], Edmund[1]

BORN: 1870
MARRIED: **Ina Maud King** (daughter of Robert).
CHILDREN: 1. **Dorothy J. (Bain) Ricker**[10]—born 1897; married **Andrew Ricker** (son of Jackson). Dorothy died in 1986. Dorothy and Andrew had 2 sons:
    (1) **James Ricker**[11]—married **Marjorie Doane** and they had two sons.
    (2) **Allan Ricker**[11]—married **Effie Davidson**. No issue.
  2. **Ernest F. Bain**[10]—born in 1898; married **Thelma MacWilliams**. Ernest died in 1972. Ernest and Thelma had one daughter:
    (1) **Carolyn Bain**[11].
  3. **Wendell William Bain**[10]—born in 1904; married **Hazel 'Madame' LeBlanc.** No issue.
  4. **Florence (Bain) Chipman**[10]—married **Harold Chipman** (1905-1975) (son of Rev.Chipman) and they had twins:
    (1) **Jean Chipman**[11]—twin of John
    (2) **John Chipman**[11]—twin of Jean; married 1st **Margot Redding** and they had:
      (i) **Jana Chipman**[12]
      (ii) **Mark Chipman**[12]
  John and Margot were divorced and he married 2nd **Sharon Cann.** John and Sharon had:
      (iii) **Cara Chipman**[12]
      (iv) **Sondra Chipman**[12].
  5. **Nathan S. Bain**[10] —born in 1908; married **Ernestine Palmer** (born 26 October,1911) (daughter of George from Kingston and Bass Corners). Nathan and Ernestine had:
    (1). **J. Natalie (Bain) Crosby**[11] -married **William Crosby**. Natalie and William had four children:
      (i) **Lynn Crosby**[12]
      (ii) **Dawn Crosby**[12]
      (iii) **Geoffery Crosby**[12]
      (iv) **Anne Crosby**[12].
    (2) **D. Lorraine (Bain) Moore**[11]—married **Douglas Moore**. Lorraine and Douglas had two children:
      (i) **Krista Moore**[12]
      (ii) **Craig Moore**[12].
    (3) **Anita Ellen (Bain) Christian**[11]—married **Terrence Christian.** Anita and Terrence had four children:
      (i) **Matthew Christian**[12]
      (ii) **Sarah Christian**[12]
      (iii) **Michael Christian**[12]
      (iv) **Emily Christian**[12]

(4) **Alexander Nathan Bain**[11]—married **Marilla Comeau** (daughter of Adolph and Madeline Comeau). Alexander and Marilla had three children:
  (i) **Marla Bain**[12]
  (ii) **Nathan Bain**[12]
  (iii) **Jessica Bain**[12]
6. **Ethel (Bain) Howell**[10]—born 1910; married **George Howell** (1907-1979). Ethel died in 1989. Ethel and George had two children:
(1) **Malcolm Howell**[11] (1932-1969).
(2) **Sharon (Howell) Tonlin**[11]—married **Anthony Tonlin.** Sharon and Anthony had two children:
  (i) **Bretta Tonlin**[12]
  (ii) **Brent Tonlin**[12]
7. **Jennie M. (Bain) Penchard**[10]—born 13 October, 1912; married **George Penchard.** Jennie died in May of 1989. Jennie and George had two daughters:
(1) **Marie (Penchard) Boutilier**[11] -married **George Boutilier** on 17 December,1954. George was born 22 June,1933 in Yarmouth and died 19 August 2004 in Ottawa, Ontario. Marie and George had two sons:
  (i) **Peter Boutilier**[12]—married **Candace Breakwell** and they had one daughter:
    (a) **Kimberly Boutilier**[13].
  (ii) **David Boutilier**[12]—born 11 February, 1956; married **Debbie Hatfield.** David died in May of 1984. No issue.
(2) **Florence (Penchard) MacDonald**[11]—married **Burton MacDonald** on 15 August, 1959. Florence and Burton had two children:
  (i) **Blair MacDonald**[12]
  (ii) **Darren MacDonald**[12]—Darren married **Wendy Dulong** on 9 May,1987. Darren and Wendy had one son:
    (a) **Chad MacDonald**[13]

information on the Nathan Bain Family courtesy of Florence (Penchard) MacDonald and Nathan S. Bain.

THE EIGHT ALEXANDER BAINS OF YARMOUTH

Alexander Bain I —born circa 1750, husband of Sarah Perry
Alexander Bain II[7]—born 1776, son of Alexander I
Alexander Bain III[8]—born 1800, son of Alexander II
Alexander Bain IV[8]—born circa 1815, son of Samuel
Alexander Bain V[9]—born 1837, son of Alexander III
Alexander Bain VI[9]—born circa 1850, son of Alexander IV
Alexander Bain VII[9]—born 1878, son of Joseph B.
Alexander Bain VIII[11]—born 1951, son of Nathan.

NOTES

CHAPTER 4
THE DESCENDENTS OF THOMAS PERRY

5th child of Moses
THOMAS PERRY[6]
son of: Moses[5], Samuel[4], Ezra[3], Ezra[2], Edmund[1]

BORN: 4 May, 1755, in Sandwich, Massachusetts.
DIED: May 1803 in the West Indies.
MARRIED: **Elizabeth Trask** (daughter of Elias) on 27 Aug.1778
                   Elizabeth was born circa 1754 and died 27 May, 1803.
CHILDREN: 1. <u>**Thomas Perry**</u>[7]—born 11 September,1779; lost at sea Dec. 1803;
                      married **Mercy Robbins** (born 1 August,1781) (daughter of Joseph)
                      at Plymouth, Massachusetts.
                   2. **Joseph Perry**[7]—born 17 May,1781, died unmarried.
                   3. **Elizabeth (Perry) Clements**[7]—born 8 October,1783; married
                      John Clements (born 2 December,1780) (son of Capt. John).
                      Elizabeth and John had 5 children. Elizabeth's nickname was
                      'Betsy'.
                   4. **William Perry**[7]—born 10 June,1786; died May 1803 in the West
                      Indies. William must have been sailing with his father when their
                      ship was lost.
                   5. <u>**John Perry**</u>[7]—born 4 October,1788; died 20 Sept.1864 and is
                      buried in Town Point Cemetery. He married **Hannah Hemeon**
                      (1792-1872) (daughter of Adam of Phillip). John and Hannah had
                      12 children.
                   6. **Eleanor (Perry) (Horton) Haskell**[7]—born 24 July, 1792; married
                      1st **William Horton** (son of Jonathan); 2nd **William Haskell** from
                      Sunderland, England .
                   7. **Mary Polly (Perry) Wyman**[7]—born 4 February, 1794; married
                      Jacob Wyman (son of Matthew) on 28 February, circa 1812. Mary
                      Polly and Jacob had 5 children:
                      (1) **Mary Eliza (Wyman) Brown**[8] —married **John Brown** (son of
                          Capt. William) in 1830. Mary died 28 February, 1854.
                      (2) **Emily (Wyman) Brown**[8]—born 1815; married **Samuel
                          Brown** (son of Capt.William) on 13 August, 1834.
                      (3) **Sophia (Wyman) Brown**[8]—born 1 December,1817; married
                          Capt. Joseph J. Brown (son of Capt.William) on 18 October,
                          1835.
                      The Wymans and the Browns must have been neighbors because all
                          three Wyman girls married Brown brothers.
                      (4) **Jacob Wyman**[8]—died young
                      (5) **Jacob Wyman**[8]—born 1827; died 1895; had
                          (i) **Jony Wyman**[9] -married and lived in Weymouth.
                          (ii) **Maria (Wyman) Sterritt**[9]—married **Capt. James A.
                              Sterritt.**

THOMAS DURING THE DAYS OF THE AMERICAN REVOLUTION

Thomas was working on board a schooner with shipmates John Trask, and Ambrose Allen under Capt. Clements. On March 20, 1776, they sailed from Chebogue bound for Halifax. On board were two passengers—Joshua Burgess and the Rev. Jonathan Scott.

On March 22, the schooner encountered a storm so it put into Liverpool. On the 23rd, a nearby man-of-war, H.M.S. Senegal which had been "impressing' men for service against the American Colonies, seized Clements' schooner and took the three crewmen aboard leaving Capt. Clements and the passengers.

Rev. Scott went to the British ship to plead for the release of the men and was successful in obtaining the freedom of Allen and Trask. However, Thomas Perry was held. Why one man was held and not the others is an interesting question but some authors think maybe because Perry was the youngest and unmarried at the time, he was a prime candidate for being "drafted".

Rev. Scott then went on to Halifax to plead for the release of Thomas Perry. Whether he was successful then, or whether Perry escaped later is not known, but 2 years after this episode, he was back in Yarmouth to marry Elizabeth Trask.

—from Gwen Trask's ELIAS TRASK, HIS CHILDREN AND THEIR SUCCEEDING RACES.

1ˢᵗ son of Thomas:
CAPT. THOMAS PERRY[7]
son of: Thomas[6], Moses[5], Samuel[4], Ezra[3], Ezra[2], Edmund[1]

BORN: 11 September, 1779.
DIED: December 1803 -lost at sea, on route from Boston to Yarmouth. Was master of the schooner '*Pilgrim*'.
MARRIED: **Mercy Robbins** (daughter of Joseph I). She later married **Elkanah Clements**
CHILDREN: 1. **Joseph Perry (Capt.)**[8]—born 12 June, 1800; died 15 April, 1864. He married **Mary (Durkee) Parry** (widow of Ebenezer), 24 November 1831.
              2. **Edward Perry (Capt.)**[8]—born 27 October,1801; died 22 February, 1870; married 1ˢᵗ **Lydia Kinney** 1803-1865 (daughter of Nathan); 2ⁿᵈ **Mary (Durkee) Perry** (widow of brother Joseph).
              3. **Elizabeth (Perry)(Kinney) Porter**[8]—born 1803; died 28 February,1854 and is buried in "Frost Park" in the town of Yarmouth. She married 1ˢᵗ **Capt. Nathan Kinney** (son of Nathan); 2ⁿᵈ **Nehemiah Porter** (son of Nehemiah), on 17 May, 1843.
              4. **Sarah Anne (Perry) Robbins**[8]—born 1804; died 2 February, 1837; married **Deacon Ansel Robbins** (son of Deacon Joseph) on 31 May, 1829.*(see page 49)*
              Note the family of sea captains: - Capt. Thomas (1755), Capt. Thomas (1779), Capt. Joseph (1800), Capt. Edward (1801)

CAPT. JOSEPH PERRY[8]

son of: Capt. Thomas[7], Thomas[6], Moses[5], Samuel[4], Ezra[3], Ezra[2], Edmund[1]

BORN: 12 June, 1800 in Yarmouth.
DIED: 15 April, 1864 and is buried in Town Point Cemetery.
MARRIED: **Mary (Durkee) Parry** (widow of Ebenezer), 24 November, 1831.
CHILDREN: 1. **Thomas James Perry (Capt.)**[9]—born 28 June, 1832; he died 24
January,1892 and is buried in Mountain Cemetery, Yarmouth. Capt.
Thomas married 1st **Janet Horton** (1824-1879) (daughter of
Benjamin) on 10 February,1863; 2nd **Loannah** ? (1839-1914). Capt.
Thomas and Janet had 2 children:
(1) **Mary Ellen Perry**[10]—born 28 March, 1865; died 1938.
(2) **Elizabeth Thomasine Perry**[10]—born 30 June,1867.

2. **William Horton Perry**[9]—born 9 December,1833; married 1st
Caroline Dunham (daughter of James); 2nd **Wealthy L. Trask**
(daughter of Samuel) 13 September, 1879. William Horton died 14
September,1896. William Horton fathered 3 children:
(1) **James William Perry**[10]—born 1855; died young.
(2) **Joseph Evelyn Perry**[10]—born 1857; died young.
(3) **Caroline Perry**[10]—born 1859; died young.

3. **Amasa Durkee Perry**[9]—born 22 February,1836; married **Sarah
Anne Robbins** (daughter of Deacon Ansel & Sarah Anne (Perry)
Robbins) on 5 Dec. 1872. *(see page 48).*

4. **Edward Robbins Perry**[9]—born 10 October,1837; married **Maria
Nickerson** (daughter of Thomas) on 16 October,1864. Edward's
professions were listed as a mariner and a farmer. Edward and Maria
had 7 children:
(1) **Charles Perry**[10]—born 1865; married and lived in Mass.
(2) **Ross Webster & Murray L. Perry (twins)**[10] - born 24 Oct. 1869;
Ross married **Nellie Leary** of Newport, R.I.
(3) **Leonora Frances (Perry) Cooper**[10]—born 10 Dec. 1870; married
James Cooper of England.
(4) **Janet Jessie Horton (Perry) Wood**[10]—born 28 Mar. 1873;
married **Arthur Wood** of Harvard Massachusetts.
(5) **Blanche T. F. Perry**[10]·-born April, 1875 in Yarmouth.
(6) **Emily G. Perry**[10]   -born 1878 in Yarmouth.

5. **Ruth Ellen Perry**[9]—born 28 June, 1839; died 17 June,1864 and is
buried in Town Point Cemetery; never married.

6. **Margaret J. (Perry) Rogers**[9]—born 22 December,1841; died 1933.
Married **Israel L. Rogers** (son of John).Margaret and Israel had 4
children:
(1) **Douglas Rogers**[10]—married **Bessie MacDonald** (New Glasgow).
(2) **Edna Rogers**[10].
(3) **J. Lovitt Rogers**[10]— died at 2 years.
(4) **Bessie Rogers**[10] —died at 9 years.

7. **Elizabeth (Perry) Crowell**[9]—born 1 January, 1844; married
Joseph Hallett Crowell (son of Capt. Hallett). Elizabeth and Joseph
had 1 child:

(1) **Annie Crowell**[10]—died in infancy.

8. **Lydia (Perry) Nickerson**[9]—born 21 March, 1846;
married **Thomas Nickerson** (son of Thomas) on 12 January,
1867. Lydia and Thomas had 1 child:

(1) **Margaret Louisa (Nickerson) Raynard**[10]—married
Gordon Raynard.

CAPT. EDWARD ROBBINS PERRY[8]
son of: Capt. Thomas[7], Thomas[6], Moses[5], Samuel[4.]. Ezra[3], Ezra[2], Edmund[1]

BORN: 27 October, 1801
DIED: 22 February, 1870 of TB and is buried in Mountain Cemetery in
              Yarmouth.
MARRIED: 1st **Lydia Kinney** (1803-1865)(daughter of Nathan II); 2nd **Mary
              (Durkee) Perry** (widow of brother Joseph). Mary is buried at Little
              River Harbour.
CHILDREN: 1. **Capt. Thomas Perry**[9]—born 1823, married: 1st **Anna Byrne**
(Lydia's)   (daughter of Thomas) on 4 October,1849; 2nd **Elizabeth Brown**
                (daughter of Capt. Robert) on 15 April, 1876.
            2. **Nathan Kinney Perry (Capt.)**[9]—born 1825; married **Maria Anna
                Durkee** (daughter of Capt. Lyman) on 20 October, 1852. Maria died
                21 September, 1913 at 87 years of age. Capt. Nathan died 2 February,
                1868 at sea. Nathan and Maria had 5 children:
                (1) **James Albert Perry**[10]—born 18 April, 1854; married **Mary
                    Booth** 13 February, 1879. James Albert died 8 June, 1897. James
                    Albert and Mary had 3 children:
                    (i) **Albert Booth Perry**[11]—born 9 October, 1881.
                    (ii) **Mary Booth Perry**[11]—born 25 August, 1884.
                    (iii) **Caribel Booth Perry**[11]—born 27 September,1885.
                (2) **William Edward Perry**[10]—married **Caribel Burrell** (1864-
                    1954) (daughter of William J. G. Burrell) on 21 June, 1887.
                (3) **Frank Lyman Perry**[10]—born in 1859 and died in 1888. He was
                    Master of the brig *Echo of Annapolis.*
                (4) **Nehemiah Ernest Perry**[10]—born 1861 and died 24 Dec.1884.
                (5) **Annie Maria Perry**[10]—born in 1865 and died 23 Jan. 1868.
            3. **Lydia Ellen (Perry) Trefry**[9]—married **Job H. Trefry** (son of
                Benjamin) 29 January,1846; died 5 March, 1895.
            4. **Edward Stephen Perry (Capt.)**[9]—born 1829; married **Eliza H.
                Crocker** (1830-1902)(daughter of David)1 January, 1858. Edward
                Stephen died 26 November,1885. Edward Stephen and Eliza had 2
                children:
                (1) **Bertha Laurena Perry**[10]—born 2 July, 1860; died 1934.
                (2) **Charles Rowland Perry**[10]—born 1 April, 1863; married **Ella
                    Phoebe Larkin** (daughter of Capt. Edward)
            5. **Prince William Perry (Capt.)**[9]—born 1831; died in the West Indies
                on 16 January, 1856; unmarried.
            6. **Lois Emily (Perry) Byrne**[9]—married **Capt. Ebenezer Corning
                Byrne** (son of Thomas) on 2 November, 1856; died 23 October, 1858.

7. **Robert Charles Perry (Capt.)**[9]—born 6 December, 1836; married **Mary S. Crocker** (1839-1929)(daughter of Daniel) on 17 April, 1863. Robert died 25 July, 1898 in Manila, Philippines. Robert Charles and Mary had 4 children:
 (1) **Maria Agnes Perry**[10]—born 4 March,1864; died 31 March, 1864 and is buried in Plymouth Cemetery, Yarmouth County.
 (2) **Carrie Eveline Perry**[10]—born April 7, 1866; died 1941.
 (3) **Robert Ernest Perry**[10]—born 1 January; married **Annie Louisa Johnson** (daughter of Capt. Cereno) on 14 June,1892.
 (4) **Nathan Gordon Perry**[10]—married **Ethel May Coosey** (daughter of Maurice of Glen Falls, New York), on 15 Jan.1897.
8. **Nehemiah Clements Perry (Capt.)**[9]—born 1839; lost at sea, 7 February, 1861; unmarried.
9 **Wentworth Kinney Perry (Capt.)**[9]—born 16 August, 1843; married **Aminilla "Amy" Steele (**1849-1889) (daughter of Charles) on 3 June, 1868. He died 18 January,1878. Wentworth Kinney and Amy had 5 children:
 (1) **Frank Chester Perry**[10]—born 22 September, 1869; married **Blanche C. Gibbons** on the 9 October, 1895.
 (2) **Charles Arthur Perry**[10]—born 4 February, 1871.
 (3) **Flora Blanche Perry**[10]—born 16 March, 1874; died 18 April, 1876.
 (4) **Leonard Ray Perry**[10]—born 22 May,1876.
 (5) <u>**Lawrence Wentworth Perry**</u>[10]—born 3 December,1877; married **Corrine Baron** on 23 April, 1921 in Boston, Mass. Lawrence died 27 May, 1952.
10. **Eliza Anne (Perry) Lawton**[9]—married **Charles L. Lawton** of Michigan on 4 November, 1869. They had four children:
 (1) **Harry Lawton**[10]—born 10 February,1871.
 (2) **John Lawton**[10]—born 10 October, 1873.
 (3) **Anna (Lawton) Bliss**[10]—born 28 October, 1875; married **William Bliss** in 1895.
 (4) **Jessie Evelyn Lawton**[10]—born 20 April, 1886.

CAPTAIN THOMAS PERRY [9]

son of: Capt. Edward[8], Capt. Thomas[7], Thomas[6], Moses[5], Samuel[4], Ezra[3], Ezra[2], Edmund[1]

BORN: 20 September,1823 at Little River, Chebogue.
MARRIED: 1st **Anna Byrne** (1831-1875) (daughter of Thomas) on 4 October, 1849;.2nd **Elizabeth Brown** (1840-1921) (daughter of Capt. Robert) on 15 April, 1876.
DIED: 13 Oct. 1900
CHILDREN: 1.**Charles Edward Perry**[10]—born 23
(Anna's)   Oct.1851; died 29 February 1852.
         2. **Anna Maria Perry**[10]—born 18 December, 1852; died 16 Jan 1853.

3. **Henry 'Harry' Heckman Perry**[10]—born 4 October, 1855; died 30 January, 1936. He married 1st **Hannah Rosella Howard** from Portland, New Brunswick on 20 December, 1887; 2nd **Annie Maria Fennell** (1859-1943) from Guelph, Ontario in 1898. Hannah Rosella died on 26 April, 1889. Harry and Annie Maria had 3 children:

(1) **Thomas Donald Perry**[11]—born in 1899; married **Annie Laura Cameron** (1901-1985) in 1926. Donald died in 1966. Donald and Annie Laura had 2 children:

   (i) **Lorne Cameron Perry**[12]—married **Grace Roberta Berry** in 1960.

   (ii) **Brian Henry Perry**[12]—married **Anna Pansy Sigler** in 1958.

(2) **Louise Marguerite (Perry) Pope**[11]—born 14 January, 1901; married **G. E. Francis Pope** from Quebec in 1922. Francis died in 1972 and Marguerite in 1989. They had 3 children:

   (i) **Kathryn (Pope) Bygate**[12]—married **Charles Bygate** in 1971.

   (ii) **Donald Francis Pope**[12]—married **Winnifred Pacey** in 1951.

   (iii) **Marjorie Anna (Pope) Schiess**[12]—married **Jacob Schiess** in 1965.

(3) **Maiben Aird Perry**[11] -born 18 October,1905; married **Mabel Anna (Porter) Mumford** in 1944. Mabel died 4 April, 1989 and Maiben died in 1972. Mabel had children from a previous marriage:

   (i) **Marilyn (Mumford) Barnes**[12]—step-daughter of Maiben, daughter of Mabel; married **Mr. Barnes.**

   (ii) **Gertrude (Mumford) Tilley**[12]—step-daughter of Maiben, daughter of Mabel; married **Mr. Tilley.**

   (iii) **Jane Diane (Perry) (Atkinson) Banks**[12]—married 1st **Carson Atkinson** and 2nd **Tom Banks**

(Elizabeth's)   4. **Anna Marguerite 'Rita' (Perry) Harris**[10]—born 24 May,1877; married **Dr. William Cecil Harris** on 16 December, 1903. Rita died 1 January, 1953.

Elizabeth (Brown) Perry-second wife of Capt. Thomas Perry. Mother of Rita

HENRY HECKMAN PERRY

Henry Heckman Perry was the third child of Capt. Thomas Perry and Anna Byrnes and was born in 1855. His middle name, Heckman, came from a friend of the family. His mother died when he was 20 years and his father married again the next year to Lizzie Brown, and within a year they had a little girl, Anna Marguerite.

Young Harry as he was called, began his schooling in the Port Maitland School but was sent off to the States to complete his education as the Oblate Seminary in Bucksport, Maine. Somewhere along the way he learned carpentry—perhaps an elementary skill that most boys were taught in those days. He evidently became skilled working with wood, because he went to sea at one point as a ship's carpenter.

He had a period of uncertain health in his twenties and the common prescription was a sea voyage. He was taken on as carpenter on one of the family-owned wooden-hulled sailing vessels—*the Lizzie Perry*. His diary of that trip to Ireland survives. This diary shows Harry's religious faith was strong and it remained so, all his life.

Home from the sea, Harry set up a carpentry shop in Port Maitland and soon specialized in carriage-making. The old shop building still stands. When the first automobiles started to appear in Nova Scotia soon after the turn of the century, they were owned by the doctors, postmen, and livery stable operators. Many arrived with nothing but chassis and motor, so it became the job of the carriage maker to apply the appropriate auto body. H.H. Perry provided this service. He also took on the Massey-Harris farm implement dealership in 1881, setting up a show room for both carriages and farm equipment in Yarmouth.

Harry Perry married twice. His first wedding, to Hannah Rosella Howard of Portland, New Brunswick took place on 20 December, 1887. She died two years later from complications resulting from a broken bone.

At a Bible Conference in Saint John , Harry met Annie Fennell from Guelph, Ontario. She was head nurse at the Stratford General Hospital. They wed in 1898 and set up housekeeping in Port Maitland. They held 'Breaking of the Bread' meetings at their home for many years, and hosted a Brethren Conference by inviting their Brethren to come to Port Maitland for three days of special meetings—no small undertaking. They rented the Odd Fellows Hall and made beds upstairs for the men by tacking sailcloth over piles of straw. Brethren came from St. John, Halifax, Montreal and New England and a happy time was had by all.

Three children were born to Harry and Annie: Thomas, named for his Grandfather Thomas; Louise Marguerite named after her mother; and Maiben Aird after well-known and respected families in the Upper Canada Brethren Assemblies. Hector Maiben was a travelling preacher of some repute and the Aird Family was well-off and noted for its philanthropic gestures.

Harry's business prospered and he built a fine new house in Port Maitland and in 1905, they moved in.

The home was Victorian in style and way of life. There was a parlour, used only for official visits and as the assembly hall, but there were plenty of other rooms where everyday family life went on.

The three children attended school in Port Maitland.

Donald became fascinated with electricity, just then in its infancy. He and his friends built crystal radio sets to pick up transmissions from passing steamers. They got a hold of an old magneto device, used for making sparks in auto engines, and wired it up to the town grump's outhouse seat. He came bellowing out of the door in an awful hurry without taking the time to pull up his drawers.

Among Don's companions in these antics were Gene and Earl Porter, whose young sister, Mabel, married Maiben Perry in 1944.

When Don finished school in 1917, the First World War was in full swing. Too young to join up, he went off to Halifax to seek his fortune in the emerging telephone business. Maritime Telephone and Telegraph hired him as a telephone installer.

He was working at the Sackville Street telephone exchange getting ready to bring it on line, when two ships, the Mont Blanc and the Imo, collided in the Harbour about two miles away with catastrophic results. The date was December 6th, 1917.

Donald moved on to North Sydney where for awhile he was a night chief tester— running tests on long distance lines. Annie Cameron was the night operator in New Glasgow and that particular trunk line was soon the best tested line on the system. In 1925, Donald and Annie each decided to move to Montreal, where they married a year later. Donald and Annie had two sons: Lorne and Brian. With the exception of two years in Toronto, Lorne has stayed in Montreal and Brian moved to Vancouver and later to Toronto

Maiben also gravitated to Montreal and in the early 1930s was a young man with a good job with Southern Canada Power Company, a car and a vigorous lifestyle; complete with spats, cream coloured gloves and homburg hat. In 1943, Maiben finally decided to settle down returning to Port Maitland to court a girl he had known from school days—Mabel Ann (Porter) Mumford—a widow for several years. Maiben took on a ready made family of two girls when he married Mabel—Gertrude and Marilyn Mumford. They lived in Montreal for a time and then moved on —Gertrude to Vancouver and later to Nova Scotia. Marilyn moved to Toronto. Mabel and Maiben had a daughter in 1946 named Jane Diane. Jane eventually moved to New Brunswick.

Marguerite was courted by a young Brethren gentleman from the Province of Quebec, Francis Pope, who met her at a Bible conference in Montreal. They were wed in 1922 at her home in Port Maitland after they had seen each other on just three occasions! They had three children: Kathryn, Donald, and Marjorie. The children went to school in Richmond, Quebec, moved to Montreal in their teens to continue their education and to seek employment. Later Don and his family moved west to Calgary.

Harry and Annie Perry, now retired from the business, closed up the Port Maitland house in the winter times and took an apartment in Montreal. During one of these winter sojourns, Harry, deaf as a door post, was struck by a car and badly injured. He died at the age of 80 in 1936. Annie continued in uncertain and failing health until 1943 when she passed away in a nursing home in Montreal.
many thanks to Lorne Perry for his fascinating contribution to the Henry Perry family

ANNA MARGUERITE 'RITA' (PERRY) HARRIS[10]
daughter of: Thomas[9], Capt. Edward[8], Capt. Thomas[7], Thomas[6], Moses[5], Samuel[4], Ezra[3], Ezra[2], Edmund[1]

BORN: 24 May, 1877
MARRIED: **Dr. William Cecil Harris** M.D.(1875-1952) on 16 Dec, 1903.
DIED: 1 January, 1953.
CHILDREN: 1 **Karl Balfour Bentley Harris[11]** - born 21 April,1907; married **Hilda May Phillips** (1907-1999) on 4 June, 1931. Karl died on 30 October, 1975 in Nova Scotia. Karl and Hilda had two children:
         (1) **Elizabeth (Harris) Kane[12]** - married **John Kane.** Elizabeth and John had three children:
             (i) **John David Kane[13]**(1962-1965)

54

(ii) **Michael Andrew Kane**[13] - who married **Karen**. Karen had a daughter from her first marriage and Michael and Karen had a son:
(a) **Amanda Kane**[14]
(b) **Kyle Kane**[14]
(iii) **Christopher Lee Kane**[13] - married **Jennifer**. Christopher and Jennifer had two children:
(a) **Zachary Kane**[14]
(b) **Noah Kane**[14]
(2) **Karl 'David' Harris**[12] - married **Winona Mary 'Nonie' Clemo**. David and Nonie had two children:
(i) **Margaret Jane (Harris) Webb**[13] - who married **Donald Alexander Webb** in 1996.
(ii) **Karl David Miles Harris**[13] - who married **Kimberly Tidd** in 1997.

2. **Dr. Herman Leander 'Hum' Harris**[11] DDS, Colonel (retired) in The Royal Canadian Dental Corp-born 27 June 1908; married **Margaret Simpson Farquharson** (1911-2010) on 27 June 1936. Hum died on 14 February 1968 in London, Ontario, Canada. Hum and Marg had two children:

(1) **Joanne Margaret (Harris) Mann**[12]-married **Charles 'Charlie' Mann**. Joanne and Charlie had three children:
(i) **Heather Margaret (Mann) Gottinger**[13]-married **Richard George Gottinger**. Heather and Richard had three children:
(a) **Derek Michael Gottinger**[14]
(b) **Caitlin Elizabeth Gottinger**[14]
(c) **Jared Christian Gottinger**[14]
(ii) **Kathryn Louise (Mann) Nan**[13] -married **Peter John Nan**
(iii) **Sharon Elizabeth (Mann) Dunn**[13] -married **Bruce Wayne Dunn**.
(2) **William Robert 'Bob' Harris**[12] -who married **Patricia 'Pat' Lockwood**. Bob and Pat had one child:
(i) **Peter Jason Harris**[13].

Many thanks to Heather (Mann) Gottinger for her information and pictures of the Capt. Thomas Perry Family

WILLIAM EDWARD PERRY[10]

son of: Capt. Nathan[9], Capt. Edward[8], Capt. Thomas[7], Thomas[6], Moses[5], Samuel[4], Ezra[3], Ezra[2], Edmund[1]

BORN: 22 September, 1857.
DIED: 8 July,1905 and is buried in Mountain Cemetery in Yarmouth.
MARRIED: **Caribel Burrell** (daughter of William John Gibson & Bethia (Allen) Burrell) on 21 June,1887. Caribel was born 3 November, 1864, and died 20 May, 1954.
CHILDREN: 1. **Jean Perry**[11]—born 13 October, 1888; died 1897.
          2. **Doris (Perry) Cann**[11]—born 12 January, 1890; died 1924 and is buried in Mountain Cemetery. Married **Hubert 'Bush' Rodolph Cann** (son of Capt. Rodolph) in December 1913.

DORIS (PERRY) CANN[11]

daughter of: William Edward[10], Capt. Nathan[9], Capt. Edward[8], Capt. Thomas[7], Thomas[6], Moses[5], Samuel[4], Ezra[3], Ezra[2], Edmund[1]

BORN: 12 January, 1890.
MARRIED: **Hubert 'Bush' Rodolph Cann** (son of Capt. Rodolph) in Dec, 1913.
DIED: in 1924 and is buried in Mountain Cemetery.
CHILDREN: 1. **Clement Park Cann[11]**—born 16 June, 1914; died 19 May, 1953 and is buried in Mountain Cemetery, Yarmouth. Clement married **Marjorie 'Marm' Cook Pettet** (daughter of G. Morton) March 1940. Clem and Marm had 2 children:
   (1) **Doris Euphemia (Cann) Zilio[12]**—Doris married **William Zilio** from Terra Cotta, Ontario on 20 April, 1963. Doris and Bill are currently (2015) living in Chatham, Ontario. They have one son:
      (i) **George William 'Billy' Zilio[13]**- George William has three children:
         (a) **Jamie Michel Zilio[14]**- Jamie's mother is **Katie Dumaine** and Jamie is currently (2015) attending university in Quebec City.
         George William married **Rhonda Dianne Walzak** on 9 July, 2004. They have two children:
         (b) **Devan William Zilio[14]**-
         (c) **Lyla Presley Zilio[14]**
   (2) **George Clement Cann[12]**—George married 1st **Cheryl Marie Sweeney** (daughter of Kenneth) in 1967 (divorced); married 2nd **Laura Elizabeth Wadman** from Glace Bay, Nova Scotia. George and Laura had three children:
      (i) **Tracey Lynn Cann[13]**.
      (ii) **Marjorie Elizabeth 'Beth' Cann[13]**.
      (iii) **Dorothy Rae Cann[13]**.
   George and Laura were divorced and he married **Carol Lynn Heustis** on 31 December, 1995. Carol passed away 7 March, 2011 and is buried in the Cann lot in Mountain Cemetery. In September 2012, George married **Patricia May (Cleveland) Baker** .
2. **Henry 'Gregg' Cann[11]**—born 1915; died 1991; unmarried. Gregg is buried in Mountain Cemetery, Yarmouth.
3. **William 'Bill' Rodolph Cann[11]**—born 1917; died 1 June,1969 and is buried in Carleton Cemetery. Bill married **Hazel Critcher.** Hazel died November 1994. Bill and Hazel had 1 son:
   (1) **Charles Cann[12]**—born 22 September,1954.; died 10 July, 2010 and is buried in the Carleton Cemetery
4 . **Jean Hope (Cann) Marshall[11]**—born 1919; died 1971 and her ashes are buried in Carleton Cemetery. Jean married **Lynn Marshall** (born in 1914). Jean and Lynn had 1 son:
   (1) **Peter Marshall[12]**
5. **Hubert 'Bush' Cann[11]**—born 1920; died 1972 and his ashes are buried in Carleton Cemetery. Hubert married **Doris Velma Nickerson**, who died in 2010. Bush and Doris had 2 children:

(1) **Richard Cann**[12]—born 5 March, 1947; died 15 November, 2001.

(2) **Wanda Cann**[12].

6. **Faith Gardner (Cann) Turnbull**[11]-born 1921(twin of Joyce). Faith married **Robert Turnbull** in March of 1943. Robert died 22 March, 2007. Faith and Robert had 2 children:

(1) **Elizabeth Gardner Turnbull**[12]

(2) **Walter Hubert Turnbull**[14] -born 18 April, 1951; died 18 June,2009

7. **Joyce Burrell (Cann)Lawrence**[11]—born in 1921 (twin of Faith); died in 2008. Joyce married **Gordon Lawrence** who died in 2005. Joyce and Gordon had 4 children:

(1) **Sandra Joyce Lawrence**[12]—born 3 April, 1942; died 30 Feb. 2001.

(2) **Anne Louise Lawrence**[12].

(3) **Faith Margaret Lawrence**[12]

(4) **Barbara Lorraine Lawrence**[12]

Many thanks to Doris (Cann) Zilio for her information on the Doris (Perry) Cann family

LAWRENCE WENTWORTH PERRY[10]

son of: Wentworth Kinney[9], Capt. Edward[8], Capt. Thomas[7], Thomas[6], Moses[5], Samuel[4], Ezra[3], Ezra[2], Edmund[1]

BORN: 3 December, 1877.

MARRIED: **Corinne Baron** (born 9 September,1890- died 6 April, 1988) on 23 April, 1921 in Boston, Massachusetts.

DIED: 27 May, 1952.

CHILDREN: 1. **Thomas Raymond Perry**[11]—born 28 April, 1922; married **Evelyn Crossman** from Montreal on 10 July,1950. Thomas Raymond died 2 April,1978. Thomas Raymond and Evelyn had two daughters.

(1) **Linda (Perry) O'Rourke**[12]—married **Daniel O'Rourke** on 28 June, 1975. Linda and Daniel had three children:

(i) **Michael O'Rourke**[13]

(ii) **Peter O'Rourke**[13]

(iii) **Sean O'Rourke**[13]

(2) **Catherine (Perry) DeBlois**[12]

2. **Alfred Lawrence Perry**[11]—born 4 December,1933; married **Thelma Marie Whitelaw** on 17 April,1954. Thelma Marie was born 1 April, 1935. Alfred and Thelma had two children:

(1) **Raymond Alan Perry**[12]—born 26 December,1954; died 19 September, 1971.

(2) **Brenda Corinne (Perry) Dahlberg**[12]

Many thanks to Linda(Perry) O'Rourke for her information on the Lawrence Wentworth Perry Family.

JOHN PERRY [7]

son of: Thomas[6], Moses[5], Samuel[4], Ezra[3], Ezra[2], Edmund[1]

BORN: 4 October, 1788.
DIED: 20 September,1864 and is buried in Town Point Cemetery.
MARRIED: Hannah Hemeon (1792-1872) (daughter of Adam of Phillip).
CHILDREN: 1. **Margery Jane (Perry) Smith**[8]—born 1822; married **Benjamin Smith** (son of Job H.); died 24 Jan.1892. They had 8 children:
      (1) **Thomas P. Smith**[9].
      (2) **Benjamin B. Smith**[9]—married **Antoinette D. Raymond** (daughter of William S.) on 29 December,1864.
      (3) **Eliza J. (Smith) Tooker**[9]—married **Thomas B. Tooker** (son of Benjamin), 3 December,1855.
      (4) **Hannah M. (Smith) Dane**[9]—married **Norman J. Dane** (son of Capt. Samuel) 18 October,1860.
      (5) **Maria K. (Smith) Goldsmith**[9]— married **George Goldsmith** of Annapolis, 31 May 1867.
      (6) **Lucy A. (Smith) Drew**[9]—married **Samuel Drew**, 22 April, 1867.
      (7) **Howard J. Smith**[9]
      (8) **Arthur Smith**[9].
   2. **Eleazer Perry (Capt.)**[8]—born 1823; married **Eliza Horton** (daughter of Capt. Robert) on 6 November, 1843. Eleazer and Eliza had 7 children:
      (1) **Julie Alice (Perry) Magray**[9]—born 1844; died 18 June, 1928 ; married **Andrew Magray** (son of Andrew).They had 9 children.
      (2) **Frank Perry**[9]—born 1846; lost at sea; unmarried.
      (3) **John Lockhart Perry (Capt.)**[9]—born 1847; married **Minnie Dunlop** in England; died in 1907.
      (4) **Henrietta (Perry) Cook**[9]—born 1849; married **Manasseh Cook** (son of Manasseh).
      (5) **Elizabeth (Perry) Sellon**[9]—born 1850; married **Mr. Sellon.**
      (6) **Almira (Perry) Butler**[9]—born 1852; married **Charles Butler** of Cardiff, Wales.
      (7) **Abigail (Perry) Johnson**[9]—born 1853; married **George Johnson** of Massachusetts.
   3. **John Perry**[8]—born 1824; married **Margaret**?
   4. **Abigail (Perry) Camplin**[8]—born 1825; married **Mr. Camplin.** The Camplins had 2 daughters:
      (1) **Melissa (Camplin) Hemeon**[9]—married **Miner Hemeon**
      (2) **Ellen M. (Camplin) Headly**[9] —was adopted by her Aunt Eleanor MacMullen. Ellen married **Isaiah S. Headly** of Wilmont, Nova Scotia, on 5 August, 1867.
   5. **Eleanor (Perry) MacMullen**[8]—born 1826; married **Capt. Joseph W. MacMullen** (son of James) on 4 Sept. 1845. Eleanor and Joseph adopted their niece:
      (1) **Ellen M. (Camplin) Headly**[9] (daughter of Abigail)
   6. **Elizabeth (Perry) MacMullen**[8]—born 1828; married **George MacMullen** (son of James) on 15 October, 1848.

7. **Maria (Perry) Hemeon**[8]—born 1832; married **John Hemeon** (son of Phillip) 30 March,1856. Maria died 18 April,1898. Maria and John has 3 sons:
   (1) **Capt. Clarence Hemeon**[9]—married **Sarah Churchill** (daughter of Stephen).
   (2) **Edgar Hemeon**[9].
   (3) **John Hemeon**[9].
8. **William H. Perry**[8]—born 1833; married **Lois Hemeon** (daughter of Phillip). William and Lois had 4 children: William died in 1863 and Lois later married **Josiah Beal.**
   (1) **Charles Perry**[9]
   (2) **Melvin Perry**[9]-married **Marietta Murphy** and they had **Caroline**[10], **Bertha**[10] and **Grace**[10]. Shortly after the 1881 census, this family moved to Cambridge, Massachusetts

   (3) **Dora Lee Perry**[9]-born 1858, died in 1927; had **Leslie Bloomfield Perry** born 1883 and died 1965. Leslie married **Rachel Margaret MacDonald** and they had 6 children, one of whom was **Kenneth Milton Perry**[10] (1926-2013). In the 1900 US census, Dora is listed as single, a tailoress, who came to the US from Nova Scotia in 1881.

Leslie B. Perry   (4) **Lillian Perry**[9]

Author's note: Kenneth Perry contacted me some years ago and was searching for his "true name" to pass on to his children. His birth certificate in Massachusetts said his surname was 'Perry'. Grandmother Dora married Edward B. Barton (date unknown) and some records show Dora's son Leslie Bloomfield (Kenneth's father) as a Barton, others as a Perry. Leslie's marriage licenses and draft cards (official records) all say 'Perry'. Kenneth's generation were all Perrys.

In the 1881 Canadian census, Dora is single. In the 1900 US census, Dora is single and living in Cambridge, MA. Her mother Lois is in the household too. In the 1910 census, Dora says she is married, but still using the Perry name. In the 1920 census, Dora says that her father was Peter B. McLoughen! In this same census, she claims she is widowed, son Leslie is living in the same household,which is headed by a 28 year old Peter B. McLoughen who Leslie says is his cousin. Sadly Kenneth passed away before any progress was made to unravel this mystery.

9. **Thomas Perry (Capt.)**[8]—born 10 November, 1832 in Yarmouth; married **Eliza Churchill** (daughter of John & Abigail (Rogers)) on 14 December, 1854 at Chebogue. Eliza was born 29 June, 1835 in Chebogue, and died 25 January, 1922 in Belmont, Massachusetts. Capt. Thomas was lost at sea October, 1870. Thomas and Eliza had 7 children:
   (1) **Charles Perry**[9]—born 10 January, 1855 at Chebogue and he was lost at sea with his father in October 1870.
   (2) **Martha M. (Perry) Hogan**[9]—born 7 October,1857 in Chebogue and she died 5 November, 1940 in Belmont, Massachusetts. Martha married on 12 October, 1876 in Yarmouth, **Thomas Ralph**

Hogan—born 18 November, 1847 in Halifax, Nova Scotia and died 12 March,1938 in Belmont, Massachusetts. Martha and Ralph had 2 children:

(i) **Thomas Errol Hogan**[10]— born 5 December,1880 in Yarmouth, Nova Scotia and died in Waltham, Massachusetts. Thomas Errol married **Ada Hurlburt** —born 7 June,1882 in Wakefield, Massachusetts and died in Waltham.

(ii) **Mary Eliza (Hogan) Simm**[10]—born 18 February, 1883 in Yarmouth, Nova Scotia and died in Bedford, Massachusetts on 30 August, 1975. Mary Eliza married **Alva Glenn Simm** on 13 August, 1913 in Belmont, Massachusetts. Alva Glenn was born 21 October, 1890 in West Gore, Nova Scotia and died 17 October, 1952 in Bedford, Massachusetts.

(3) **Ida May (Perry) Perry**[9]—born 16 August, 1859 in Chebogue; married **Capt.Wellington W.Perry**[8] (son of Thomas of Elisha) *(see page 85)* on 10 July,1878. Ida May died in British Columbia. They had 3 children:

(i) **Staley Perry**[10]—born in 1879 at Chebogue. Staley never married and he died in British Columbia.

(ii) **Martha May Perry**[10]—born 23 April, 1883 in Chebogue. She never married and died 22 May, 1990 at 107 years of age in Chebogue.

(iii) **Verna (Perry) Schell**[10]—born 13 May,1886 in Chebogue; married **Ed Schell**. They had no children. Verna died 6 March, 1989 in Kelowna, British Columbia at age 103 years.

(4) **George Gordon Perry**[9]—born 3 August, 1862 in Chebogue; married **Alice Cook** (1861-1938) from Bridgewater, Nova Scotia. George Gordon died in 1925 and is buried in Belmont, Massachusetts. They had no children.

(5) **William Edgar Perry**[9]—born 17 October,1864 in Chebogue. William Edgar never married and died 29 January,1927 in Mass.

(6) **Ellen Heatley (Perry) Moody**[9]—born 20 June, 1868 in Chebogue; married **Harry R. Moody** (son of Ralph) on 24 October, 1892 . Ellen died in Newcastle, New Brunswick. They had one son:

(i) **Ralph Victor Moody**[10]—died in Worcester, Massachusetts.

(7) **Alvin Perry**[9]—born 10 June,1870 in Chebogue; married **Sarah MacCoy** of Cambridge, Massachusetts and they had one daughter. Alvin died 19 October,1930, probably in Cambridge, Mass.

10. **Foster Perry**[8]—born 1839; married **Louisa Trask** (daughter of Samuel) 20 June,1859. Foster and Louisa had 9 children:

(1) **Clement M. Perry**[9]—born 1861; died 17 Feb,1865; age 4 years, 2 months.

(2) **Lizzie L.Perry**[9]—born in 1864; died 20 June, 1865; age 9 months

(3) **Clement Perry**[9]—born 1869; died 7 Oct.1877; age 8 years, 2 mons.

(4) **Chauncey Perry**[9]—born in 1871; died 20 Nov.1871, age 10 mons.

(5) **Chauncey Perry** [9]—born 4 July, 1873; died at age 12 years.

(6) **Ralph Perry**—married in U.S.A.

(7) **Adelbert Perry**[9].

(8) **Georgina Perry**[9].

(9) **Louisa Perry**[9].

11. **Lockhart Perry**[8]—born 1841; lost at sea.

12. **Edward Perry**[8]—born 1843; died 10 July 1856; unmarried.

THOMAS ERROLL HOGAN[10]

son of: Martha (Perry) Hogan[9], Thomas[8], John[7], Thomas[6], Moses[5], Samuel[4], Ezra[3], Ezra[2], Edmund[1]

BORN: 5 December, 1880\81 in Yarmouth, Nova Scotia.

MARRIED: In 1901, **Ada Hurlburt** who was born 7 June, 1882 in Wakefield, Massachusetts. Ada died in Waltham, Massachusetts. Thomas and Ada had 10 children:

DIED: In Waltham, Massachusetts

CHILDREN: 1. **Gwendolyn Harrault (Hogan) Frude**[11]—born 11 November, 1901 in Yarmouth; married **Ed Frude**. They had one daughter:
(1) **Muriel Frude**[12]

2. **Harry Moody Hogan**[11]—born 18 September,1902 in Yarmouth; married **Beulah Stacey**. Harry died in Lexington, Massachusetts. Harry and Beulah had 2 sons:
(1) **Douglas Erroll Hogan**[12]
(2) **Carl M. Hogan**[12]

3. **Thomas Erroll Hogan**[11]—born 27 March, 1904 in Boston, Massachusetts; married **Alexis** . Thomas and Alexis had 2 children:
(1) **Sarah Hogan**[12]
(2) **Thomas Hogan**[12]

4. **Mildred Goudey (Hogan) Roberts**[11]—born 30 June, 1907 in Boston. Married **Jack Roberts**.

5. **Mary Elizabeth Hogan**[11]—born 27 September,1908 in Dorchester, Mass.

6. **Alice Perry Hogan**[11]—born 28 July, 1910 in Waltham, Mass.

7. **Douglas Selkirk Hogan**[11]—born 15 January, 1913 in Waltham, Massachusetts; died April 1992 in Naples, Florida.

8. **Ada Hogan**[11]—born in Waltham, Massachusetts.

9. **Louise (Hogan) Wheeler**[11]—born in Waltham, Massachusetts; married **Ed Wheeler**.

10. **Ruth (Hogan) Harrington**[11]—born in Waltham, Massachusetts; married **Howard Harrington**.

MARY ELIZA (HOGAN) SIMM[10]

daughter of: Martha (Perry) Hogan[9],Thomas[8], John[7], Thomas[6], Moses[5], Samuel[4], Ezra[3], Ezra[2], Edmund[1]

BORN: 18 February, 1883 in Yarmouth, Nova Scotia.

MARRIED: **Alva Glenn Simm** on 9 August, 1913 in Belmont, MA. Alva Glenn was born 21 October, 1890 in West Gore, Nova Scotia and died 17 October, 1952 in Concord, Massachusetts. Alva Glenn was a manager.

DIED: 30 August, 1975 in Lexington, Massachusetts

CHILDREN: 1. **Eunice Perry (Simm) Howe**[11]—born 24 April, 1918 in Waltham, Mass.; married **Henry Dunster Howe** on 9 February, 1946 in Belmont, Mass. Eunice was a lawyer and Henry an oral surgeon. Henry died January, 1982 in Belmont, Mass. Eunice and Henry had 2 children:

    (1) **Eunice Dunster (Howe) Amey**[12]—married **Ralph Amey** on 21 June, 1986 in Belmont. Eunice was a professor. There were no children.

    (2) **Maryalice Boardman (Howe) DOI**[12]—born in Boston; married **Lt. Col. Alan Joseph DOI** February, 1992 in Maryland. Maryalice had one son:

        (i) **Nathaniel Boardman Mauer**[13]—born in Omaha NE.

2. **Helen Simm**[11]—born 27 September, 1924 in Waltham, Mass. Helen never married and she died 23 April, 1967 in Carlisle, Mass.

3. **Miriam Beaver (Simm) Brown**[11]—born 22 March, 1927 in Arlington, Mass.; married **John Fremont Brown, Jr.** (son of John Fremont and Louise Catherine (Kirkegaard)) on 8 November, 1952 in Belmont, Mass. John was born 27 January, 1924 in Concord, Mass. Bea was a social worker and John a teacher. They had 2 children:

    (1) **Martha Susan (Brown) Healy**[12]—born in Concord, Mass.; married **Dr. James Michael Healy** (son of James Leo Jr. & Alice Catherine (Riley)) on 8 July, 1978 in Bedford, Mass. James Michael was born in Boston. Martha Susan was a nurse-educator. Martha Susan and James Michael have 3 children:

        (i) **James John Healy**[13]—born in Wareham, Mass.

        (ii) **Matthew Brown Healy**[13]—born in Newton, MA.

        (iii) **Abigail Laura Healy**[13]—born in Norwich, CT.

    (2) **John Fremont Brown III**[12]—born in Concord, Mass.; married **Dorothy Louise Marks** (daughter of George C. & Elizabeth (Leete)) on 5 September, 1982 in Fayetteville, New York. John Fremont is an engineer and Dorothy Louise a geologist. They have 2 children:

        (i) **Andrew Tyler Brown**[13]—born in Newton, Mass.

        (ii) **Elizabeth Miriam Brown**[13]—born in Newton, Mass.

4. **Alva Glenn Simm, Jr.**[11]—born 18 January, 1929 in Arlington, Mass.; married **Marion Ogilvie** on 23 June, 1955 in Belmont, Mass. Alva was a manager and Marion a nurse. Alva and Marion had 3 children:

    (1) **Lisa (Simm) Mazzeo**[12]—born in Boston; married **John Mazzeo** in May, 1989 in Waterville, Maine. Lisa is a nutritionist and she and John have one daughter:

        (i) **Elizabeth Simm Mazzeo**[13]—born in Waterville, Maine.

    (2) **Alva Glenn Simm II**[12]—born in Boston.

    (3) **Nancy Simm**[12]—born in Boston. Nancy is a teacher.

-information on the Thomas Perry Family courtesy of Miriam Beaver (Simm) Brown

CHAPTER 5
DESCENDENTS OF NATHANIEL PERRY

7th child of Moses
NATHANIEL PERRY[6]
son of: Moses,[5] Samuel[4], Ezra[3], Ezra[2], Edmund[1]

BORN: 24 June, 1759 in Sandwich, Massachusetts.
MARRIED: 1st **Lydia Tinkham** (daughter of Edward) on 3 May,1787. Lydia was
                  born in 1765 and died 8 July, 1795.
               2nd **Sarah Dennis** (daughter of Capt. Ambrose) on 1 May,1798.
CHILDREN: 1. **Lydia (Perry) Pitman**[7]—born 8 February, 1788;
 (by Lydia)   married **John Pitman** (son of Benjamin).
           2. **Abigail (Perry) Johnson**[7]—born 23 January,1790 married **Daniel
              Johnson** (son of Seth) of Ohio, Yarmouth County.
           3. **Nathaniel Perry**[7]—born 20 September,1791; died in 1855; married
              Hannah Baker (daughter of Jonathan) . Hannah was born 2 Feb. 1797.
           4. **Rebecca (Perry) Hilton**[7]—born 28 April, 1794; died 26 November,
              1891; married **Capt. Nathan Hilton** (son of Thomas) in 1817.
 (by Sarah) 5. **Sarah (Perry) Holmes**[7]—born 26 February,1797; married **Joseph
              Holmes** (son of Nathaniel). Sarah and Joseph had 2 children:
              (1) **Alice Holmes**[8]—died 7 January,1831 at age 8 years.
              (2) **William Holmes**[8]—became a sergeant in the U.S. Army. He died in
                  June 1863.
           6. **Mary (Perry) Everett**[7]—born 27 November,1798; married **James
              Everett** of Digby County, Nova Scotia.

LYDIA (PERRY) PITMAN[7]
daughter of: Nathaniel[6], Moses[5], Samuel[4], Ezra[3],Ezra[2], Edmund[1]

BORN: 8 February, 1788.
MARRIED: **John Pitman** (son of Benjamin I)
CHILDREN: 1. **Abiah (Pitman) Landers**[8]—born 24 July, 1814; married **Samuel
              Perry Landers** (son of Joseph) on 21 January, 1852.
           2. **William Nelson Pitman**[8]—born 8 December, 1815; married 1st
              Mary Ann Whitehouse (daughter of Joseph) on 8 October, 1848;
              and 2nd **Ellen King** (daughter of William) . Ellen died on 25
              Nov.1900.
           3. **Lydia Pitman**[8]—born 17 August, 1817; died unmarried.
           4. **Clement Pitman**[8]— lost at sea March 1844.
           5. **Eunice (Pitman) Saunders**[8]—married **Enoch Saunders** (son of
              Moses) on 17 October,1854.
           6. **John Pitman**[8]—died in1840; unmarried.
           7. **Abigail Pitman**[8]—died unmarried.
           8. **Joseph Pitman**[8]—born December 1831; married **Margaret Crosby**
              (daughter of Isaiah) on 17 April,1859. Joseph died 2 September,
              1898
           9. **Nathaniel Pitman**[8]—born in 1834; died 4 Jan.1900; unmarried.

10.**Benjamin Pitman**[8]— born in 1823; married 1st **Mary E. Head** on 12 December,1850; and 2nd **Anne Slate**. Benjamin died 19 April, 1896.

NATHANIEL PERRY[7]
son of :   Nathaniel[6], Moses[5], Samuel[4], Ezra[3], Ezra[2], Edmund[1]

BORN: 20 September,1791 on Perry's Island.
MARRIED: **Hannah Baker** (daughter of Jonathan). Hannah was born 2 Feb. 1797.
DIED: At sea of yellow fever in 1855. He was buried at sea.
CHILDREN: 1. **Jonathan Perry**[8]—born 27 August,1816; married **Margery Jane Harris** (daughter of Nathaniel Tale George) on 3 October,1841. They had a daughter:
(1) **Margery Perry**[9]
  2. **John Perry**[8]—born 29 September, 1818; married **Elizabeth Hilton** (1821-1908) (daughter of Stephen I). John died 30 December 1882 and is buried in Carleton Cemetery.
Around 1840, a Mr. Raymond built a mill in the center of where the present village of Carleton is located. (The village was first named Temperance). A year later, Raymond was followed to Temperance by the Hilton Family, the Dennis Family, the Crawley Family, and the John Perry Family.

John Perry built his first home near the lake north of the mill and on a road which would come to bear his name—the Perry Road. The site of this Perry house was across the road and slightly north of the entrance of the current YMCA Camp, while the barn was located near the Camp's present entrance.
John and Elizabeth had 10 children:
(1) **Stephen Perry**[9]—born 1840; married **Mary A. Crosby** (1844-1918) (daughter of Deacon Nathan of James of James). Stephen died in 1918 and is buried in Riverside Cemetery. Stephen and Mary had 3 children:
  (i) **Laliah (Perry) Bain**[10]—married **Benjamin Raymond Bain***(see page 32)*
  (ii) **John M. Perry**[10] (1873-1941)—married **Maude Winter** (1870-1937) (daughter of William). John M. and Maude had a daughter:
    (a) **Nita Joyce Perry**[11] (1910-1927).
  (iii) **Farwell Perry**[10] (1875-1910).
(2) **John Perry**[9]—born in 1842; lost at sea.
(3) **William Perry**[9]—born in 1845.
(4) **Elizabeth A. (Perry) Rose**[9]—born in 1851; married **George M. Rose** (son of John I) on 12 May, 1871.
(5) **Thomas H. Perry**[9]—born 1 September, 1852; died 2 Sept. 1852.
(6) **Thomas H. Perry**[9]—born 1854; married 1st **Ada Eldridge** (daughter of Richard), and 2nd married **Louisa Eldridge** (daughter of Richard).

(7) **Norman J. Perry**[9]—born in 1855; married **Harriet Goudey** (daughter of John). Norman was accidently shot and killed at Winthrop, Massachusetts on 19 October, 1899.

(8) **Alva (Perry) Harding**[9]—born in 1857; married **Robert Harding.**

(9) **Ella M. Perry**[9]—born 20 Sept.1860; died 9 March,1882; unmarried.

(10) **Nathaniel Perry**[9]—married **Ida Farquharson.**

3. **Capt. Nathaniel Perry**[8]—born 8 December,1819. He married **Tabitha Crawley** (daughter of Edmund) on 17 April,1850 and they had 1 son:

(1) **Clarendon Perry**[9]—died unmarried

4. <u>**Lydia (Perry) Richardson**</u>[8]—born 28 October, 1821; married **Samuel Richardson** (son of David). Lydia died 20 January, 1885.

5. <u>**Nathan Perry**</u>[8]—born 25 September,1823; married **Caroline Dennis** (daughter of Capt. Leonard of Amos I of Ambrose) on 18 Sept. 1848. Lydia was born 16 January,1824 and died in 1906. Nathan died 16 Sept.1865.

6. **James Perry**[8]—born 16 January,1825; died at 4 years of age.

7. **Capt. Samuel Perry**[8]—born 2 November,1827; married **Mary D. Crosby** (1835-1914) (daughter of Capt. Lemuel) on 4 January, 1855. Capt. Samuel died in 1887. Samuel and Mary had 9 children:

(1) **Charles Perry**[9]—born 1856; died in 1884.

(2) **Mary Perry**[9]

(3) **Alice Perry**[9]

(4) **Sarah Perry**[9]

(5) **Isabella (Perry) Colpitts**[9]—married **Parker Colpitts** of Halifax, Nova Scotia. Isabella and Parker had 3 children:

  (i) **Marjorie B. Colpitts**[10]—unmarried

  (ii) **Mildred (Colpitts) Reed**[10]—married **Dr. Alan Reed** of Halifax

  (iii) **Merle (Colpitts) Bronson**[10]—married **Prof. (Dr.) D.L. Bronson.**

Cemetery records also show:

(6) **Sadie M. Perry**[9]—1861-1879.

(7) **Amy C. Perry**[9]—1868-1868.

(8) **W. Eva Perry**[9]—1871-1879.

(9) **Bernard W. Perry**[9]—1879-1879.

8. **Hannah (Perry) Miller**[8]—born 25 March, 1829; married **Joseph Miller** (son of Isaac*) (see pg. 87)* on 29 November,1852. They had 9 children:

(1) **Mary (Miller)(Roy) (Foss) Wyman**[9]

(2) **George G. Miller**[9] —married **Minnie Strowe**

(3) **Howard Miller**[9]—married **Ms. Meadowcroft**

(4) **Oscar D. Miller**[9]—married **Alice George**

(5) **Josephine (Miller) Elliott**[9]—married **Perry Elliott**

(6) **Grace Maud Miller**[9]

(7) **Edward Miller**[9]—died young

(8&9) two other children were born to Hannah and Joseph.

9. **Rebecca (Perry) Smith**[8]— born 5 May,1831; married **James Smith** (son of Capt. Obed). Rebecca and James had 2 children:

(1) **Clarissa (Smith) Cook**[9]—who married **Stephen Cook** (son of Francis G.)

(2) **Joel Munroe Smith**[9]—who died at 4 years of age.

10. **Sarah Emma (Perry) Benjay**[8]—born 18 August,1832; married **Barry Benjay** on 13 June, 1875.

11. **Mary E. (Perry) Crosby**[8]—born 6 April,1834; married **Capt. John B. Crosby** (son of Lemuel) on 24 May, 1860. Mary died July 1898. Mary and John had 4 children:
    (1) **Lemuel Staley Crosby**[9]—married **Althea Hines** (daughter of Caleb).
    (2) **Annie B. (Crosby) Blauvelt**[9]—married **Frederick Blauvelt** (son of Capt. Robert) in 1884.
    (3) **Thomas C. M. Crosby**[9]
    (4) **Cornelius Crosby**[9]—born in 1870; married **Miss Hatfield** (daughter of John V.N.)
12 **James Perry**[8]—born 22 October, 1835; married **Emma Turner** (daughter of John I).
13. **Joel Perry**[8]—born in 1837; lost at sea.
14. **Martha (Perry) Cain**[8]—born 27 April,1840; married **James Cain** (son of Capt. Seth). Martha died 27 February, 1886. Martha and James had 1 child:
    (1) who died at an early age
15. **Anne (Perry) Cain**[8]— born 18 June,1842; married **Samuel Cain** (son of Capt. Seth) on 8 December, 1861. Anne and Samuel had 5 children:
    (1) **Stanley Cain**[9] —married 1st **Ethel Spinney** and 2nd **Sadie (Cook) Cunningham** (widow of Hartley) (daughter of Stephen Cook). Stanley had one son:
        (i) **Lloyd Cain**[10]—married 1st **Mildred Wilson** of Barrington Passage, Nova Scotia and 2nd **Inez Eldridge.**
    (2) **James Cain**[9]—born 1862; married **Annie Miller** (1865-1904). James died in 1935.
    (3) **Martha (Cain) Skinner**[9]—married **Joseph Skinner** of Middleton, Nova Scotia.
    (4) **Burton Cain**[9]—married **Elizabeth Healy.**
    (5) **Mabel (Cain) Hogg**[9]—married **Henry Hogg.** Mabel died 19 Oct.1900

LYDIA (PERRY) RICHARDSON[8]
daughter of: Nathaniel[7], Nathaniel[6], Moses[5], Samuel[4], Ezra[3], Ezra[2], Edmund[1]

BORN:	28 October, 1821
MARRIED:	**Samuel Richardson** (son of David). Samuel was born in April of 1815, and died 17 January,1916 at age 101 years.
DIED:	20 January, 1885.
CHILDREN:	1. **Hannah (Richardson) Bain**[9]—born 8 February,1844; married **Samuel A. Bain**[9] *(see page 31)* (son of William) on 2 August, 1873. Hannah died in 1880.
	2. **Nathaniel Richardson**[9]—born 21 November,1845; married **Harriet Patterson** (daughter of Thomas).
	3. **Mary (Richardson) Major**[9]—born 25 March,1847; married **William Major.** Mary died in July of 1882.
	4. **Charles B. Richardson**[9]—born 4 December,1849; married **Alice (Miller) Hilton** (widow of Stephen). Charles died 20 Sept.1881.
	5. **Lydia (Richardson) Nicholl**[9]—born 24 April,1854; married **William Alnutt Nicholl** (son of William) on 31 July, 1873. Lydia died 4 June,1930.

6. **Tabitha (Richardson) Bain**[9]—born 14 April, 1856; married **Samuel A. Bain** (son of William and widower of sister Hannah) *(see page 31)* on 19 October, 1881.

7. **Susanna (Richardson) Crosby**[9]—born 5 December,1859; married **Thomas Allen Crosby** (son of Capt. David) in 1879. Susanna died 2 July, 1948 at 89 years.

NATHAN PERRY[8]

son of: Nathaniel[7], Nathaniel[6], Moses[5], Samuel[4], Ezra[3], Ezra[2], Edmund[1]

BORN: 25 September, 1823.

MARRIED: **Caroline Dennis** (daughter of Capt. Leonard of Amos) on 18 September, 1848. Caroline was born 3 November,1823 in Yarmouth and died 6 August, 1906.

DIED: 16 September,1865. Both Caroline and Nathan and son Frederick T. are buried in Carleton Cemetery, Yarmouth County.

CHILDREN: 1. **Alice Jane Perry**[9]—born 28 June,1849; died 21 September, 1850.

             2. **Leonard William Perry** [9]—born 13 January,1851; died 5 April, 1851.

             3. **Capt. Frederick Tompkin Perry**[9]—born 14 April,1852; died in 1925; married **Joanna Randall** (daughter of David).

             4. **Alice Jane Perry** [9]—born 10 January,1854; died 16 June,1858.

             5. **Leonard William Perry**[9]—born 18 April,1856; died 28 June,1858.

             6. **Nathan Douglas Perry**[9]—born 30 April,1858; died 6 March, 1944; married **Emma Maud Hurlburt** (daughter of William) on 8 October, 1881. Emma was born on 1 November,1860. Nathan Douglas died 6 March,1944. Nathan Douglas and Emma Maud had 7 children:
               (1) **Arnold V. Perry**[10]
               (2) **Mabel D. (Perry) Goodrich**[10]—married **H. Goodrich**
               (3) **Alice J. (Perry) Smith**[10]—married **Frank Smith.**
               (4) **Roy C. Perry**[10]
               (5) **Anna R. Perry**[10]
               (6) **Florence Perry**[10]
               (7) **Nettie W. Perry**[10]

             7. **Freeman James Perry**[9]—born 25 June 1860 in Carleton, NS; died 17 June, 1943 in Thunder Bay, Ont. He married **Antoinette Maud Robbins** (1861-1938)(daughter of Chandler) on 11 October, 1883.

             8. **William Albert Perry**[9]—born 19 August, 1862; died in 1917; married 1st **Alice Gardner,** and 2nd **Marian 'Minnie' Adams.** William fathered 4 children:

(by Alice)   (1) **Arthur Perry**[10]—married **Melissa Wood.** In 1910, they moved from Massachusetts to Ontario, Canada and then on to Winnipeg, Manitoba.

               (2) **Carl C. Perry**[10]—died young.

(by Marian) (3) **Esther L. Perry**[10]

               (4) **Elenor Hazelwood (Perry) Monroe**[10]—married **James Albert Munroe** on 27 September,1924. They had three children:
               (i) **Dana Osborn Munroe**[11]—born 21 February 1928.
               (ii) **Bruce Munroe**[11]—born 21 December, 1930.
               (iii) **Albert Dana Munroe**[11]—born 15 June,1932.

9. <u>**Caroline Augusta (Perry) Nickerson**[9]</u>—born 26 June, 1864; died in 1924; married **Summer Troup Nickerson.**
10. <u>**Arthur Franklin Perry**[9]</u>—born 13 May, 1866 in Carleton, Yarmouth County; died 21 December, 1941 in Jacksonville, Florida; married **Isabelle Cowan Strawn.** Arthur and Isabelle had 2 children:
   (1) **Arthur Franklin Perry II**[10].
   (2) **Henry Strawn Perry**[10].

ARTHUR FRANKLIN PERRY [9]—BANK PRESIDENT

Arthur was born after his father's death and was brought up by an uncle—Freeman Dennis. At age 15, Arthur left Yarmouth Academy and went to work in his uncle's business—Vilts & Dennis, Importers and Dealers in Dry Goods.

In 1884, Arthur left Yarmouth and ventured to Jacksonville, Florida where he found employment with the Atlantic Railroad as a cashier. From cashier, he was promoted to bookkeeper and after several years, Arthur left the railroad and joined the State Savings and Trust Company as a cashier. This Savings and Trust Company was reorganized into the Mercantile Exchange Bank and Arthur progressed up the ranks to vice-president. In 1913, he became president of the Mercantile Exchange Bank.

Arthur was active in the community in which he lived with his family. He was an organizer of the Boy Scouts in Jacksonville; was a trustee of the Jacksonville Library; was State Treasurer for the United War Campaign in 1914; and was treasurer for the Roosevelt Memorial Association.

-Who's Who in American History

CAPT. FREDERICK TOMPKIN PERRY[9]

son of: Nathan[8], Nathaniel[7], Nathaniel[6], Moses[5], Samuel[4], Ezra[3], Ezra[2], Edmund[1]

BORN: 14 April, 1852.
MARRIED: **Joanna Randall** (daughter of David from Kemptville, Yarmouth County)
DIED: 1925 and is buried in Carleton Cemetery.
CHILDREN: 1. **Emma Caroline Perry**[10]—born 20 October, 1880; died in 1892.
   2. **Albert Vandella Perry**[10]—born 10 August, 1882; killed in Milwaukee while at work 9 January, 1909.
   3. **Violet May (Perry) Hurlburt**[10]—born 5 April, 1884; married **Wallace Hurlburt** (son of George) on 5 April, 1904; died March of 1954. Violet and Wallace had 8 children.
   4. **Vera Genevieve (Perry) (Dyer) Boyle**[10]—born 7 March 1886; married 1st **E. Dyer** and 2nd **William Boyle.** Vera had three children.
   5. **Blanche Lillian (Perry) Mackereth**[10]—born 13 February, 1888; married **William W. Mackereth** on 20 October, 1910. Blanche and William had three children:
      (1) **Irene (Mackereth) Cooper**[11]—married **Lloyd Cooper.**
      (2) **Albert Mackereth**[11]—married **Esther Hanson**
      (3) **Perry Mackereth**[11]—married **Anne Hatchen.**

6. **Jonathan Osborne Perry**[10]—born 11 June, 1890; killed in action during World War I while serving in France, 12 June, 1917. His name can be found on the Soldier's Memorial Monument in the park at Carleton.

7. **Abigail 'Abbie' Dennis (Perry)(Howard) Stone**[10]— born 21 September, 1891; married 1st **John Howard** and they had three children; married 2nd **J. Stone**. Abigail died 15 September,1947.

8. **Balfour St. Clair Perry**[10]—born 13 February, 1893; married 1st **Miss Perry** and they had three children; married 2nd **Mamie?** and married 3rd **Lillian Rice**. Balfour died 20 November, 1969 in Framingham, MA.

9. **Emily Caroline 'Lina' (Perry) Mackereth**[10]—born 9 April, 1895; married **Stanley Mackereth** on 26 June, 1930; no children.

10. **Evoira Frauline Perry**[10]—born 13 July,1897; died at 12 days of age .

11. **Frederick Russell Perry**[10]—born 12 December,1900; married **Hester Flood** in June 1928. Frederick and Hester had 6 children.

12. **Harley Edon Perry**[10] —born 16 December,1902; married **Phyllis Mill** on 21 October, 1948. Harley died 7 July,1973 in Victoria, British Columbia.

FREEMEN JAMES PERRY[9]

son of: Nathan[8], Nathaniel[7], Nathaniel[6], Moses[5], Samuel[4], Ezra[3], Ezra[2], Edmund[1]

BORN: 25 June, 1860.
MARRIED: **Antoinette M. Robbins** (daughter of Chandler) on 11 October, 1883.

Family tradition said that Freeman was raised by an aunt, whom he called "Long John Silver". In the 1881 census he is listed as a school master. Freeman moved his young family to Fort William ,Ontario from Yarmouth in 1888 where he worked as a switchman for the C.P.R. railroad. In 1894, they moved to Slate River, where they homesteaded and Freeman became the first teacher in the new Slate River Valley school. The 1901 census show him as a farmer. After 23 years living in the Slate River area they moved on to Port Arthur where Freeman worked as a timekeeper for the Port Arthur Shipyards. In 1919, they bought land in Hurkett where Freeman operated a grocery store, became a justice of the peace, and was also a timber contractor selling lumber to the Milton Francis Lumber Company. Freeman and Antoinette celebrated their Golden Wedding anniversary in 1933.

DIED: 17 June, 1943 in Thunder Bay, Ontario
CHILDREN: 1. **Nathan Maurice Perry**[10]—born 1885; drowned on 11 July, 1907.

2. **Ida Cleveland (Perry) Miller**[10]—born 13 July,1886; married **Joseph Miller**.

3. **Phillip Carleton Perry**[10]—born in 1889; married **Muriel Kelly**.

4. **Alvin Ernest Perry**[10]—born 1890, accidently shot on 22 Jan. 1912.

5. **William Robbins Perry**[10]—born 1892; married **Laura Hughes**. William died 16 December,1961.

6. **Lewis Alan Perry**[10]—born 20 November, 1893; married **Marjorie Ramsay** (daughter of Frank David) at Los Angeles, California on 6 October,1920. Lewis and Marjorie had 2 children:

(1) **Alan Ramsay Perry**[11]—born 10 October, 1921; lived in Kelso,
Washington; died 18 Aug. 2005. Married **Judith Ann Job.**

(2) **Patricia Antoinette (Perry) Bradley**[11]—born 2 April, 1924
and lived in Kelso, Washington. Married **Wilbur Farrell
Bradley, Jr.** on 23 March, 1943 in La Mesa, California
*The wedding had been originally set for earlier in the year, but
Pat postponed the ceremony until her brother returned from the
Front. Alan did arrive in the nick of time wearing uniform and
combat boots.----from Patricia (Perry) Bradley*

7. **Margaret and Christina** (twins) **Perry**[10]—born 2 January,1895.
Margaret died in San Bernardino, California on 19 February, 1935.
Christina died young.

8. **Douglas Perry**[10]—born 12 August, 1897.

9. **Ernest John Perry**[10]—born 1898; married **Mary Hanson**. Was a
farmer.

10. **Helen Catherine Perry**[10]—born 1899; died young.

11. **Stephen C. Perry**[10]—born in 1902; married **Martha Boyle**.
Stephen died accidently in January 1933.

12. **Marion Caroline (Perry) Aylward**[10]—born in 1906; married
Robert Aylward.

CAROLINE AUGUSTA (PERRY) NICKERSON[9]

daughter of: Nathan[8], Nathaniel[7], Nathaniel[6], Moses[5], Samuel[4], Ezra[3], Ezra[2],
Edmund[1]

BORN: 26 June, 1864.
MARRIED: **Summer Troup Nickerson**.- (1864 -1935).
DIED: 1924.
CHILDREN: 1. **Gordon Arnold Nickerson**[10]—born 10 January,1889; married
Margaret Doane in January 1914. Gordon died in 1957.

2. **Pearle Dennis Nickerson**[10]—born 1891; died 1900.

3. **Elizabeth May 'Bessie' (Nickerson) Lloyd**[10] —born 6 August, 1892;
married **Douglas Lloyd**; no children.

4. **Alice Blanche Nickerson**[10]—born in November 1894; died in 1900.

5. **Nellie Gertrude (Nickerson)(Purdy)(Bower) Kimball**[10]—born 7
September, 1896; married 1st **John Purdy** in 1917. John died in 1928.
Nellie married 2nd **Roy Bower**; and 3rd **Hayford Kimball**.

6. **Minnie B. (Nickerson) (Clements) Hilton**[10] —born 10 June, 1899;
married 1st **Alfred Clements** (son of Elkanah) on 11 March, 1920; and
2nd married **Edgar Hilton** (son of James).

7. **Annie Mildred (Nickerson) Falt**[10]—born 4 February, 1900; married
Henry Falt. Annie died in 1928.

8. **Walter LeRoy Nickerson**[10]—born 30 September 1902; married
Myrtle Brayne.

9. **William Summer Nickerson**[10]—born 27 March, 1905; married **Eva
Wood.**

10. **Carrie Viola Nickerson**[10]—born 9 September,1908; died 1924.

11. **Rita (Nickerson) Pizer**[10] –born circa 1912; married **Israel Isaac Pizer** in 1928. Rita died in 1990 in Arizona.

REBECCA (PERRY) HILTON[7]
daughter of: Nathaniel[6], Moses[5], Samuel[4], Ezra[3], Ezra[2], Edmond[1]

BORN: 28 April, 1794.

MARRIED: **Capt. Nathan Hilton I** (son of Thomas I) in 1817. Capt. Hilton died 16 May, 1853.

DIED: 26 November, 1891.

CHILDREN:
1. **Wentworth Hilton**[8]—born 5 October, 1817; married **Eunice Dennis** (daughter of Capt. Amos). Wentworth died in San Jose, California on 27 February, 1853.
2. **Nathan Hilton**[8]—born 9 September, 1819; married 1st **Martha Crosby** (daughter of Ebenezer II) in 1840; 2nd married **Eleanor J. Brown** (daughter of Amos B.) in 1877. Nathan died 30 August, 1895.
3. **Herbert Hilton**[8]—born 22 November,1821; married **Frances Hibbert** (daughter of David).
4. **Charles Hilton**[8]—born 16 September,1823; married **Elizabeth Mary Haley** (daughter of Joseph E.) on 18 January, 1848.
5. **Stephen Hilton**[8]— born 15 August,1825; drowned at Carleton on 23 August, 1839.
6. **Thyrza (Hilton) Miller**[8]—born 23 July,1829; married **John P. Miller** (son of Isaac) on 28 December, 1855.
7. **George Hilton**[8]—born in 1833; died in 1838 at age 5 years.
8. **David Hilton**[8]—born in 1835.
9. **Amos Hilton**[8]—born 24 July,1837; married **Margaret Kelley** (daughter of Daniel) on 14 December,1859.

Clara (Burridge) Perry on way to her murder trial
Page 80

The Jean (Perry) Corning Family
Page 95

CHAPTER 6
ANNA (PERRY) CLEMENTS

8TH child of MOSES
ANNA (PERRY) CLEMENTS[6]
daughter of :   Moses[5], Samuel[4], Ezra[3], Ezra[2], Edmund[1]

BORN: 6 September,1761, three months after the family sailed to Nova Scotia.
               Anna has the distinction of being the first English child born in the new
               township of Yarmouth.
               There is an interesting tale passed down through the Perry
       generations which states that Anna was born under an apple tree on the
       family farm. This family legend may be based in fact, since Campbell's
       History states that Moses spread tenting material over an apple tree on the
       farm and this was their first dwelling.
MARRIED: **Capt. Silas Clements** (son of John) on 21 December,1784. They were
               married by the Rev. Jonathan Scott
DIED: 14 January, 1846; buried in Town Point Cemetery, Chebogue next to
               Silas.
CHILDREN: Anna and Silas reportedly raised a nephew of hers, **Joseph Ellis**, son of
               Anna's sister, **Rebecca** and **Phillip Ellis**.

Anna (Perry) Clements
— *from the Yarmouth Historical Museum*

Ray and Gladys Palmer
page 97

Ina & Fred Perry's Wedding
page 94

Kenneth Milton Perry
page 59

Melitta Jane (Bain) Clements
and daughter Daisy Gladys
page 38

CHAPTER 7
DESCENDENTS OF ELISHA PERRY

9th child of MOSES
ELISHA PERRY[6]
son of: Moses[5], Samuel[4], Ezra[3], Ezra[2], Edmund[1]

BORN: 1765
MARRIED: **Sarah Perry** of Cape Negro, Nova Scotia. Sarah died 4 March,1856 at age 92 years.
DIED: Town Point Cemetery tombstone reads:
In Memory of Elisha Perry who departed this life 29 Oct.1828 in his 65 year.

CHILDREN: 1. **Rufus Perry[7]**—(twin of Anna); born 4 March, 1789.
2. **Anna (Perry) Landers[7]**—(twin of Rufus); born 4 March,1789; married **Thorndyke Landers** (son of Jabez). Anna died in 1879 at 90 years of age. Anna and Thorndyke had 5 children:
   (1) **Elisha Perry Landers[8]**—married **Matilda MacQuinn** of Liverpool, Nova Scotia on 28 January, 1847.
   (2) **Cynthia (Landers) Griswold[8]**—born in 1814; married **Capt. Emery Griswold** of Cape Negro. Cynthia died 1 November, 1866.
   (3) **Elizabeth (Landers) Marling[8]**—married **Barnet Marling** (son of Barnet).
   (4) **Zilpha (Landers) Jeffery[8]**—born in 1824; married **Joseph Jeffery** (son of Archibald). Zilpha died 4 July, 1852 and is buried Yarmouth's "Frost Park" which was the "Old Town Cemetery".
   (5) **Rachel (Landers) Pitman[8]**—married **Capt. Richard Pitman** (son of Joseph).
3. **Sarah (Perry) Landers[7]**—born 21 August,1791; married **Thomas Landers** (son of John) and they had 4 children. Sarah died 5 June, 1863.
4. **Abigail Perry[7]**—born 12 November,1793; died 4 January,1833.
5. **Alfred Perry[7]**—born 28 April, 1795; married **Catherine Perry** (daughter of William of Cape Negro). Alfred and Catherine had 7 children:
   (1) **Sarah Ann Perry[8]**
   (2) **Sophronia Perry[8]**
   (3) **Benjamin Perry[8]**
   (4) **Hiram Perry[8]**—married **Welthea Anne Pitman** (daughter of William) on 24 July, 1865.
   (5) **Foster Perry[8]**
   (6) **Margaret Perry[8]**
   (7) **George Perry[8]**

6. **Elizabeth (Perry) Pitman**[7]—born 20 June, 1797; married **William Pitman** (son of Joseph) on 14 July, 1830. They had 8 children. Elizabeth died 22 December, 1890. William died 21 November, 1874.

7. **Leonard Perry**[7]—born 28 October, 1798; married **Mary Hammond**(1801-1888) (daughter of William). Leonard died 11 November,1865. Leonard and Mary had 10 children:
   (1) **Elima (Perry) Murphy**[8]—born 16 July, 1822; married **Melgar Murphy** (son of James) on 12 January, 1846.
   (2) **Lucinda Perry**[8]—born 16 April, 1824; died in 1844 at age 20 .
   (3) **William Nelson Perry**[8]—born 13 December,1825; married in England.
   (4) **Elizabeth Mary (Perry) Cook**[8]—born 13 February, 1826; married **Walter Cook** (son of Caleb I) on 28 September, 1853.
   (5) **Ruth H. (Perry) (Crowell) Horton**[8]—born 7 January, 1830; married 1st **Capt. Hallet Crowell** (son of Thomas) on 23 November, 1854, and 2nd **Benjamin Horton** (son of Capt. Robert) on 12 February, 1863.
   (6) **Harriet H. (Perry) Hersey**[8]—born 5 September, 1832; married **Daniel Hersey** (son of Zador) on 19 August, 1855.
   (7) **Catherine Perry**[8]—born 27 November, 1834; died in California, unmarried.
   (8) **Amanda (Perry) Steadman**[8]—born 14 September, 1838; married **William Steadman** on 6 March, 1866.
   (9) **Oliver P. Perry**[8]—born 20 March, 1841; lost at sea with the schooner *"Charles"* off Turk's Island in June of 1855 (*Yarmouth Shipping, p. 158*).
   (10) **Frederick Hammond Perry**[8]—born 20 February, 1844; married **Helen Sophia Perry**[8] (daughter of Thomas) on 1 September, 1867.

8. **Abigail Perry**[7]—born 24 August, 1801; died 25 June, 1885.

9. **Thomas Perry**[7]—born 25 May , 1804; married 1st **Sophia Walker** (daughter of Joseph); 2nd **Olive Scott.**

10. **Zipha (Perry) Trefry**[7]—born 17 January,1806; married **William A. Trefry** (son of Joshua P. II) on 16 August, 1827. Zipha died in 1875.

11. **Sophronia (Perry) Crosby**[7]—born 17 May,1809; married **Capt. Foster Crosby** (son of Deacon John). Foster died 20 April, 1857. Sophronia and Foster had 8 children:
   (1) **Hannah Kelley (Crosby) Marshall**[8]—born in 1830; married **Samuel Marshall** (son of Edward) on 19 January, 1853.
   (2) **Emily Jane (Crosby) Cain**[8]—born in 1838; married **Stephen Cain** (son of James II) on 26 June, 1861.
   (3) **Caleb Cook Crosby**[8]—born in 1840; married **Amy Hooper** of Antwerp in 1862. Caleb died 27 October, 1864.
   (4) **Foster Stanton Crosby**[8]—born in 1843; married **Edith Stowe** (daughter of Capt. Thomas) in 1870. Foster died 17 June,1886.
   (5) **George A. Crosby**[8]—born in 1845; married **Carrie Wyman** (daughter of James W.) .
   (6) **James Edgar Crosby**[8]—born in 1847; married **Margaret Kennedy** of Glasgow, Scotland. James died in 1874.

(7) **Marietta A. (Crosby) Crosby**[8]—born in 1849; married **Anthony J. Crosby** (son of Freeman) in 1866.

(8) **Louisa M. (Crosby) Drysdale**[8]—born in 1855; married **Arthur W. Drysdale** in 1877.

Descendents of RUFUS PERRY[7]
1st son of Elisha Perry
son of: Elisha[6], Moses[5], Samuel[4], Ezra[3], Ezra[2], Edmund[1]

BORN: 4 March, 1789 (twin of Anna).
MARRIED: **Susan Porter** (daughter of George Dudley)
DIED: 1834.
CHILDREN: 1. <u>**James Albert Perry**</u>[8]—born 16 October,1816; married **Annie White**.
2. **Alfred Perry**[8]—born 1818; drowned at a young age.
3. **Caroline (Perry) Pitman**[8]—born 24 August,1820; married **Thomas Pitman** (son of Oliver) on 23 February, 1843. Caroline and Thomas had 4 children:
(1) **Rufus Pitman**[9]—born 17 May, 1844; married **Lois Jane Murphy** (daughter of Joseph) on 8 June, 1867.
(2) **Isaiah Pitman**[9]—born 13 February, 1847; died in Santa Cruz, California on 26 February, 1876.
(3) **David Pitman**[9]
(4) **Susanna Pitman**[9].
4. <u>**George Hay Perry**</u>[8]—born 22 December, 1822; married **Eliza Jane Raynard** in November 1849.
5. **Charles Alfred Perry**[8]—born in 1827; married **Phoebe Elizabeth Corning** (1832-1854) (daughter of Ebenezer) in December 1850; and they had one child:
 (1) **Helen M. Perry**[9]—born in 1852; died in 1854 at age 2 years and is buried in the Beaver River Cemetery.
Charles Alfred died in 1853 at sea aboard the schooner *"Active"* bound from Santa Domingo to New York.
6. **Abigail Perry**[8]—born 1824. She died young.
7. **Thomas William Perry**[8]—born 2 February,1832; married **Helen S. Cody** on 23 January, 1871. Thomas and Helen had 7 children:
(1) **Medley Thomas Perry**[9]—born 15 February,1873.
(2) **James William Perry**[9]—born 10 April,1874.
(3) **Frank D'Arcy Perry**[9]—born 22 December,1875; died 28 Jan. 1876.
(4) **Caroline Eugene Perry**[9]—born 8 September, 1877.
(5) **Maebel Adelaide Perry**[9]—born 25 October, 1879.
(6) **Charles Frederick Perry**[9]—born 8 August, 1881.
(7) **George Stanley Perry**[9]—born 21 November, 1886.

JAMES ALBERT PERRY[8]

son of: Rufus[7], Elisha[6], Moses[5], Samuel[4], Ezra[3], Ezra[2], Edmund[1]

BORN: 16 October, 1816.

MARRIED: **Annie White**

CHILDREN: 1. **George H. Perry**[9]—born 11 October, 1842; married 1st **Ellen J. Gillespie**, 2nd **Margaret Myers.** George fathered 4 children:

(by Ellen)   (1) **Alfred Perry**[10].

             (2) **Minnie Perry**[10].

             (3) **Josephine Perry**[10].

(by Margaret)   (4) **Charles Perry**[10.]

2. **Charles A. Perry**[9]—born 12 Aug.1844; went to California in 1875.

3. **Amos S. Perry**[9]—born 12 May, 1847; married **Caroline Jones** of Chelsea, Massachusetts. Amos and Caroline had one son:

     (1) **Amos S. Perry**[10]—who lived in East Boston.

4. **Mary Jane (Perry) Burtt**[9]—born 11 November, 1849; married **John R. Burtt**. Mary Jane and John 4 children:

     (1) **Maria A. Burtt**[10].

     (2) **John R. Burtt II**[10].

     (3) **William C. Burtt**[10].

     (4) **Arthur W. Burtt**[10].

5. **James Alfred Perry**[9]—born 1 May,1852; married **Adelaide Fulton.** James Alfred and Adelaide had 6 children:

     (1) **Beulah Perry**[10].

     (2) **Roscoe Perry**[10].

     (3) **Edith Perry**[10].

     (4) **Duncan Perry**[10].

     (5) **Ernest Perry**[10].

     (6) **Elizabeth Perry**[10].

6. **Lemuel Wilmont Perry**[9]—born 10 March,1856; married **Augusta Knox**. Lemuel Wilmont and Augusta had 5 children:

     (1) **Cora Perry**[10]—born 28 August, 1900. Cora taught school for 37 years and in 1994 was residing in a Chatham, New Brunswick nursing home. She never married.

     (2) **Russell Perry**[10]—born 1902; married **Myrtle Corcoran** in 1930; died in 1968.

     (3) **John Perry**[10] —born in 1903. John adopted;

        (i) **George Perry** in 1942. George died in 1962.

     (4) **Gordon Perry**[10]—born in 1904; died in 1992; never married.

     (5) **Edith Perry**[10]—born in 1910 and was living in Chipman, New Brunswick. Edith had one daughter :

        (i) **Helena Perry**[11]—who died in infancy.

7. **Annie E. (Perry) Black**[9]—born 2 April, 1860; married **N.D. Black** on 6 November, 1886. Annie and N.D. had 4 children:

     (1) **Otto R. Black**[10]—born 6 November 1888.

     (2) **Harry W. Black**[10]—born 1 July, 1890.

     (3) **Albert S. Black**[10]—born 11 July, 1893

     (4) **Leon L. Black**[10]—born 25 October, 1894.

RUSSELL PERRY[10]

son of: Lemuel Wilmont[9], James Albert[8], Rufus[7], Elisha[6], Moses[5], Samuel[4], Ezra[3], Ezra[2], Edmund[1]

BORN: 1902
MARRIED: **Myrtle Corcoran** in 1930
DIED: 1968
CHILDREN:
1. **Paul Russell Perry**[11]—born in 1931; married **Jennie Mabey**. Paul died in 1987.
2. **Arnold John Perry**[11]—born in 1932. Arnold married **Stella Gallant** and had four daughters:
   (1) **Darlene (Perry)McLaren**[12]—married **Rick McLaren** and had one daughter:
      (i) **Jill McLaren**[13]
   (2) **Carolyn (Perry) Hume**[12]
   (3) **Gayle (Perry) Davis**[12]—married **Mr. Davis** (since divorced) and they had two daughters:
      (i) **Rebecca Davis**[13]
      (ii) **Ashley Davis**[13]
   (4) **Janice (Perry) Miller**[12]
3. **Marion Ann (Perry) Johnston**[11]—married **William Wayne Johnston** in 1966, and lives in Waterloo, Ontario.

Information on the Lemuel and Russell Perry Families courtesy of Marion Johnston

CAPT. GEORGE HAY PERRY[8]

son of: Rufus[7], Elisha[6], Moses[5], Samuel[4], Ezra[3], Ezra[2], Edmund[1]

BORN: 22 December, 1822
MARRIED: **Eliza Jane Raymond** (1830-1882)(daughter of William S.) in November 1849.
DIED: 1902 and is buried in Mountain Cemetery
CHILDREN:
1. **Seretha Ada (Perry) Goudey**[9]—born September 1853; married **Arthur Goudey** (son of Capt. Aaron); died 10 January, 1947 and is buried in Mountain Cemetery. Seretha and Arthur had 2 children:
   (1) **Nellie Goudey**[10]—born 28 May,1882
   (2) **William Raymond Goudey**[10]—born in 1883.
2. **Capt. George Henry Perry**[9]—born 10 March, 1855; married **Clara Elizabeth Burridge** (daughter of James and Clara A. of London, England) on 12 April, 1888. George died on 26 February,1921 and has the dubious distinction of being the victim of one of Yarmouth's unsolved murders.
3. **Rodolph Perry**[9]—born 11 February, 1857; married **Louisa M. Fisk** (daughter of Robert) on 10 December,1887. Rodolph and Louisa had 6 children:
   (1) **Charles Albert Perry**[10]—born 9 January1891.
   (2) **Seretha Hazel Perry**[10]—born 10 January,1893.
   (3) **Norah Alice Perry**[10]—born 14 April,1895.
   (4) **George H. Perry**[10]—born 30 November,1896.

(5) **Elsie Graden & Laurier Raymond** (twins) **Perry**[10]—born 13 December, 1898.
   4. **Eliza Alice Perry**[9]—born 8 November, 1859; died in infancy.
   5. **Charles Perry**[9]—born 20 June, 1865. Charles sailed from Boston on the ship *Magellan,* 10 May, 1890, and was never heard of again.

CAPT. GEORGE HENRY PERRY[9]
son of: Capt. George Hay[8], Rufus[7], Elisha[6], Moses[5], Samuel[4], Ezra[3], Ezra[2], Edmund[1]

BORN: 10 March, 1855
MARRIED: **Clara Elizabeth Burridge** (daughter of James J. and Clara Burridge of London, England) on 12 April, 1888.
DIED: 26 February, 1921. Murdered by blows from a heavy iron pole on his own back porch on Argyle Street in Yarmouth.
CHILDREN: 1. **Clara Eliza (Perry) Matheson**[10]—born 6 August, 1889; married **Mr. Matheson,** and was living in New Hampshire when her father was killed.

Wife Clara

   2. **Florence Evangeline Perry (Dr.)**[10]—born 2 March, 1892; became a medical doctor; died 19 April, 1966.
   3. **Caroline Alice Perry**[10]—born 5 October, 1895, was a teacher in the Western part of Canada.
   4. **Eleanor (Perry) Ross**[10]—married **Mansfield Ross;** moved to British Columbia and years later took her own life.

THE UNSOLVED MURDER OF CAPT. GEORGE HENRY PERRY
   It was on a cold, snowy evening of February 25,1921 when Capt. Perry was struck down by several blows to the head while on the back porch of his ancestral home at 99 Argyle Street. His wife, Clara, was in the house at the time of the crime but stated she heard nothing. Perry was alive when found by his daughter's fiancee, Mansfield Ross, but died several hours later (at 1:20AM on February 26, 1921) without gaining consciousness.
   There were several very puzzling facts about this case. First of all, Capt. Perry tried to defend himself as evidenced by the bruises on the back of his hands and arms. Therefore, he must have also cried out. A neighbour did hear some shouts at about the time the murder could have taken place but he took these noises to be skaters having fun on a nearby brook. Mrs. Perry who was just a few feet away from the crime scene, quietly playing solitaire, heard nothing. After Mansfield discovered the bleeding and semi-conscious Capt. Perry, no attempt was made to move or protect him from the cold. The Captain remained outside in the snow bank where he had fallen while his wife, daughter, future son-in-law, and two neighbours sat in the kitchen sipping tea for the hour it took for Doctor Webster to arrive from Parade Street. Also it was noted that Mrs. Perry scrubbed the kitchen floor several times after 11:30 PM when the dying man was brought into the house, and Ross continued to stoke up the furnace which was not a common practice in the late evenings.

The relationship between Ross and Capt. Perry varied with the article being read, but the general consensus was that Mansfield Ross had moved into the Perry home that very day much to Capt. Perry's dismay. He would not give his permission for Eleanor to marry Ross who was part Negro and Perry was known to be a very bigoted man.

On April 19th, Mrs. Perry was arrested for murdering her husband and Mansfield Ross was charged with assisting a murderess to escape justice. She and Mansfield were held at the jailhouse on Main Street, and the trial was held in the Brunswick Street curling rink. Evidence at the trial indicated that Captain Perry did have a will but no trace of it was ever found. The trial ended in August of 1921 and Mrs. Perry and Ross were found not guilty. Clara inherited the Captain's money and property and Ross married Eleanor. Mrs. Perry sold the family home and moved to California never to be heard of again.
From Yarmouth Vanguard Feb. 9.1996 and 'A Matter of Mayhem'

Descendents of LEONARD PERRY[7]
son of: Elisha[6], Moses[5], Samuel[4], Ezra[3], Ezra[2], Edmund[1]

BORN: 28 October, 1798
MARRIED: **Mary Hammond**
CHILDREN :Leonard and Mary had 10 children.(*see pg. 76*) Their youngest child was :

FREDERICK HAMMOND PERRY[8]
son of: Leonard[7], Elisha[6], Moses[5], Samuel[4], Ezra[3], Ezra[2], Edmund[1]

BORN: 29 February, 1844.
MARRIED: **Helen Sophia Perry** (daughter of Thomas) on 1 September,1867. *(see page 85)*
DIED: February 1939 at age 95 years
CHILDREN: 1. **George Herman Perry**[9]—born 16 August, 1868; married **Cora Belle Burton** of Dorchester, Massachusetts on 16 April, 1894. George died 9 January, 1947 in Los Angeles, California. George Herman and Cora Belle had at least 3 children:
     (1) **Blanche Burton Perry**[10] —born 22 July, 1895.
     (2) **Helen Minerva Perry**[10]—born 29 February, 1898.
     (3) **Muriel Lucille Perry**[10] – born 1906 and died in 1991.
  2. **Alice Sophia (Perry) Hilton**[9]—born 28 June,1870; married **Arthur F. Hilton** of Rockville, Yarmouth County on 5 June, 1897.They had a daughter:
     (1) **Marion Louise Hilton**[10] - born 30 March,1899.
  3. **Isabelle Beatrice (Perry) Damon**[9]—born 5 October, 1872; married **Mr. Damon**.
  4. **Bertha Maude Perry**[9]—born 20 July,1874; died 16 March, 1879.
  5. **Florence Stella Perry**[9]—born 15 November,1876; died 16 March, 1879.
  6. **Jessie May Perry**[9]—born 12 January, 1881; died 1919.
  7. **Ella Horton Perry**[9]—born 18 June, 1883; never married.
  8. <u>**Lawrence Chester Perry**</u>[9]—born 23 February, 1886; married **Ellen Kenney**; died 11 July, 1971.

LAWRENCE CHESTER PERRY[9]

son of: Frederick H.[8], Leonard[7], Elisha[6], Moses[5], Samuel[4], Ezra[3], Ezra[2], Edmund[1]

BORN: 23 February, 1886.
MARRIED: **Ellen J. 'Ellie' Kenney**
DIED: 11 July, 1971.
CHILDREN: 1. <u>**Walter Emerson Perry**</u>[10]—born 3 September, 1912; married **Ruth Barnard Lewis.**
                      2. **Margaret Winifred (Perry) Maberley**[10]—born 3 May, 1914; married **Alexander Earl Maberley** on 23 July, 1942. Margaret Winifred and Alexander Earl had two children:
                          (1) **Perry Ellen (Maberley) Hurlbert**[11]—married **Jerry Arthur Hurlbert** on 2 August, 1965; since divorced. Perry Ellen and Jerry Arthur had one daughter:
                              (i) **April Marlene Hurlbert**[12]—April Marlene has a daughter :
                                 (a) **Samantha Ashley Steeves**[13]
                          (2) **Larry Alexander Maberley**[11]—married **Emily Mary Robicheau** on 26 July, 1968. Larry Alexander and Emily Mary had two children:
                              (i) **Lawrence Earl Maberley**[12]
                              (ii) **Melanie Dawn Maberley**[12]

WALTER EMERSON PERRY[10]

son of: Lawrence Chester[9] ,Frederick H.[8], Leonard[7], Elisha[6], Moses[5], Samuel[4], Ezra[3], Ezra[2], Edmund[1]

BORN: 3 September, 1912. Walter's family still live on part of the original Moses Perry land.
MARRIED: **Ruth Barnard Lewis** (born 24 December, 1908, died 13 March, 1977). Walter and Ruth were married 25 June, 1936.
DIED   22 Sept. 2004 in Chebogue, Nova Scotia.
CHILDREN: 1. **Ronald Frederick Perry**[11]—married **Gloria Ilene Swim** on 7 September, 1968. Ronald and Gloria had one son:
                          (1) **Andrew Scott Perry**[12]
                      2. **Virginia Helen (Perry) Kleiner**[11]married **Anton Kleiner** on 19 August, 1960. (divorced 22 August, 1988). Virginia Helen and Anton had five children:
                          (1) **Ruth-Anne Virginia (Kleiner) Lawrence**[12] - married **Sheridan Lawrence** on 24 September, 1988. Ruth-Anne and Sheridan had two children:
                              (i) **Garet Blaine Lawrence**[13]
                              (ii) **Lauren Ariel Lawrence**[13]
                          (2) **Janice Elaine Kleiner**[12]— (twin of Judith Ellen).
                          (3) **Judith Ellen (Kleiner) Giacomin**[12]— (twin of Janice Elaine); married **Victor Giacomin** on 30 August, 1986.
                          (4) **Mark Anton Kleiner**[12]—married **Nancy Goodwin** on 10 December,1988. Mark and Nancy had two sons:
                              (i) **Evan Mark Kleiner**[13].

(ii) **Jordan Adam Kleiner**[13]

(5) **Wendi Marie Kleiner**[12]—. Wendi Marie has a son :

(i) **Glenn Logan Surette**[13]

3. **Douglas Gordon Perry**[11]—married **Zella Mary Rose** (daughter of Bernard from Dayton, Nova Scotia) on 22 July,1961.
Doug and Zella had two children:

(1) **James Douglas Perry**[12].

(2) **Susan Marie (Perry) Works**[12]—married **Randy Works** on 8 August, 1987. Susan Marie and Randy had three children:

(i) **Anastasia Works**[13]

(ii) **Keith Douglas Works**[13]

(iii) **Jacob Bernard Aaron Works**[13]

4. **Dr. Robert Walter Perry**[11]—married **Edith Mary Riedal** (daughter of Arthur Winnin) on 30 September, 1972. Robert and Edith Mary had three children:

(1) **Candice Mary Ruth Perry**[12]

(2) **Charmaine Margaret Rose Perry**[12]

(3) **Justin Walter Arthur Perry**[12]

5. **Thomas Henry Perry**[11]- married **Hazel Lillian Churchill** on 18 July,1964. Thomas Henry and Hazel Lillian had five children:

(1) **Philip Thomas Perry**[12].

(2) **Wade Alvin Perry**[12]—born 11 September,1967; died 7 April,1971.

(3) **Monica Dawn (Perry) Malone**[12]— (adopted); married **Christopher Olin Malone** on 8 April, 1989. Monica and Christopher had one daughter:

(i) **Amanda Christine Malone**[13]

(4) **Trevor Daniel Perry**[12]—Trevor and his common law wife, **Karen Annette Chase**, had one child:

(i) **Krista Danielle Perry**[13]

(5) **Brock Tyler Perry**[12]

6. **Rosalie Ruth (Perry) Selwyn-Smith**[11]—married **Keith David Selwyn-Smith** on 27 August, 1966; divorced 26 January, 1982. Rosalie Ruth and Keith David had two children:

(1) **Heather Diane Selwyn-Smith**[12]

(2) **Michael Bryan Selwyn-Smith**[12]—born 8 Aug. 1968; died 12 July, 1991.

(information on the Lawrence C. and Walter E. Perry Families courtesy of Ronald Perry)

DESCENDENTS OF THOMAS PERRY
4t[h] son of ELISHA PERRY

THOMAS PERRY[7]
son of: Elisha[6], Moses[5], Samuel[4], Ezra[3], Ezra[2], Edmund[1]

BORN: 25 May, 1804.
MARRIED: 1st **Sophia Walker** (daughter of Joseph); 2nd **Olive Scott** (widow of James Flavel).

"Mrs. Thomas Perry (Olive) age 70, lost her life when their home in Chebogue was destroyed by fire. Her husband was attending the funeral of Samuel Trask at the time of the fire" – Yarmouth Newspaper

CHILDREN:(by Sophia)
1. **Joseph Foster Perry[8]**—born in 1827; married **Mary A. Vickery** (1838-1913)(daughter of William of Moses of Moses I) on 4 October, 1860. Joseph Foster died in 1902 and all the family except Gertrude are buried in Mountain Cemetery.
   (1) **Gertrude (Perry) Burrill[9]**—born 8 February,1862; married **George H. Burrill** (son of Samuel) in December 1887.
   (2) **Edward L. Perry[9]**—born 22 September,1865; died young in 1874.
   (3) **Sophia Walker Perry[9]**—born 23 March, 1867; died young in 1873.
   (4) **Martha Huntington Perry[9]**—born 3 Nov.1869; died young 1873.
   (5) **Anna Foster Perry[9]**—born 30 January,1875; died young in 1879.
2. **John W. Perry[8]**— born in 1828; went abroad and lost touch with family.
3. **James Albert Perry[8]**—born in 1830; died 30 June, 1836
4. **Rebecca (Perry) (Wheeland) Smithers[8]**—married 1st **Samuel Wheeland**; and 2nd **John Smithers** of California. John died in California on 21 October,1888.
5. **Thomas Perry[8]**—went abroad.
6. **Lydia Perry[8]**—died young.
7. **James Albert Perry[8]**—married **Rosanna Gates** (daughter of James of Cumberland County, Nova Scotia). James Albert died in 1893. James Albert and Rosanna had 7 children:
   (1) **James Forman Perry[9]**—born 19 May, 1867; married **Grace Goodwin** (daughter of Jeffery from East Pubnico) on 20 Sept,1892.
   (2) twins—born in 1869; died in infancy.
   (3) **John Perry[9]**—born 10 February, 1872.
   (4) **Thomas Perry[9]**—born 14 August, 1874.
   (5) **Leonard Perry[9]**—born 12 September, 1878.
   (6) **Eleanora Perry[9]**—born 24 August, 1880.
8. **Lydia S. (Perry) Blethen[8]**—married **James Blethen** on 29 Oct.1859.
(by Olive)
9. **George Henry Perry[8]**—born in 1841; died 13 June, 1862; unmarried.
10. **Sylvanus Perry[8]**—born in 1843; died in Havana, Cuba on 22 Oct. 1859.

11. **Helen Sophia (Perry) Perry**[8]—married **Frederick H. Perry**[8] (son of Leonard) on 16 September, 1867. *(see page 81)*

12. **Capt. Wellington Whitfield Perry**[8]—married **Ida May Perry**[9] (daughter of Capt. Thomas and Eliza (Churchill) Perry, son of John I). *(see page 60)* . They moved to Alberta. Capt. Wellington and Eliza had 5 children:

   (1) **Sylvanus B. Perry**[9]—born 14 November, 1879.

   (2) Infant Son—born 15 March, 1881; died in infancy.

   (3) **Martha May Perry**[9]—born 25 April, 1882.

   (4) **Bertha Annie Perry**[9]—born 10 February, 1885; died 29 Aug.1886.

   (5) **Verna Louise Perry**[9]—born 13 April, 1887.

NOTES

CHAPTER 8
DESCENDENTS OF LEVI PERRY

10th child of MOSES
LEVI PERRY[6]
son of: Moses[5], Samuel[4], Ezra[3], Ezra[2], Edmund[1]

BORN: 1766 in Yarmouth, Nova Scotia

MARRIED: **Susanna Magray** (daughter of Capt. John Magray who came from Scotland) on 21 May, 1792. Susanna was born in 1774 in Marblehead, Massachusetts and died 12 Nov. 1855 in Yarmouth, Nova Scotia. The couple was married by the Rev. Jonathan Scott. After Levi's death, Susanna married Capt. Samuel Ellis.

DIED: 6 June 1814 in Yarmouth, Nova Scotia

CHILDREN: (all 8 children were born in Yarmouth)

1. **John Magray Perry[7]**—born 2 April, 1793; died 20 October,1805 and is buried in Town Point Cemetery.
2. **Moses Perry[7]**—born 21 July,1794; married **Mercy Smith** of Barrington Passage on 13 December, 1820. Moses died 11 March,1852.
3. **Susannah (Perry) Landers[7]**—born 2 September,1798; married **Joseph Landers** (son of John from Yarmouth). They had 9 children.
4. **Rowland Briggs Perry[7]**—born 20 October,1800; died unmarried.
5. <u>**Samuel James Perry[7]**</u>—born 6 August,1802 in Yarmouth; married **Mary Margaret Brown** (daughter of Eunice (Doty) and Robert Brown); settled in Cape Negro, Nova Scotia.
6. **Elizabeth (Perry) Wyman[7]**—born 4 July,1805; married **Asahel Wyman** (son of James from Yarmouth). Asahel died in 1868. Elizabeth and Asahel had 8 children:
   (1) **Susan Wyman[8]**—born in 1829; died in infancy.
   (2) **James Wyman[8]**—married **Adelaide Saunders** (daughter of Rufus) on 20 December, 1860.
   (3) **Levi Wyman[8]**—born 28 December, 1832; married **Lois J. Landers** (daughter of Joseph) on 4 March, 1855.
   (4) **Mary Eliza Wyman[8]**—died 31 May, 1850.
   (5) **Susan Wyman[8]**—died 5 August, 1851.
   (6) **Druscilla (Wyman) Porter[8]**—born 21 November, 1838; married **Capt. Charles W. Porter** (son of Capt. Joseph) on 3 Sept. 1859.
   (7) **Daniel C. Wyman[8]**—born in 1841; died 28 March,1861 at age 20
   (8) **William Wyman[8]**—born 1843; died 22 August,1865 at 22 years .
7. **John Magray Perry [7]**—born 30 October,1807; settled in Cape Negro, Nova Scotia.
8. **Mary Ann (Perry) Miller[7]**—born 1809 or 1810; married **Isaac Miller** (1807-1883)(son of Adam). Mary Ann died in 1874. Isaac's second marriage was to **Joanna (Dukeshire) Turpin** (widow of Henry). Mary Ann and Isaac had 13 children:
   (1) **Joseph Miller[8]**—born 29 June,1829; married **Hannah Perry[8]** *(see pg. 65)*(daughter of Nathaniel) on 29 November, 1852. Hannah was born at Chebogue on 3 March, 1829.

(2) **Deborah Miller**[8]—born 1833; died in December of 1856 at age 23; never married.

(3) **Elkanah C. Miller**[8]—born 1834; died 2 June,1855 at 21 years of age.

(4) **John P. Miller**[8]—married **Thyrza Hilton** (daughter of Capt. Nathan) on 28 December, 1855. John died 14 April,1893.

(5) **Mary Anne 'May' Miller**[8]—born 1838; died 13 January, 1909; unmarried.

(6) **Reuben Clements Miller**[8]—born 1839; married **Sarah J._?** (1840-1920). Reuben died in 1902.

(7) **Elizabeth (Miller) Hardwick**[8]—married **Adelbert Hardwick** from Annapolis on 24 March,1865.

(8) **Susan (Miller) Durkee**[8]—born 1841; married **Ammiel 'Mile' R. Durkee** (son of Joseph). They had no children. Susan died 24 February, 1901 at 60 years of age.

(9) **Marie (Miller) Hilton**[8]—born 21 March 1842; married **Albert Hilton** (son of Smith) on 18 January,1862. Marie died 31 January, 1905.

(10) **William H. Miller**[8]—born 28 June, 1844; married **Mary Hilton** (daughter of Smith) on 3 January, 1868. William died 21 June,1900 at 56 years of age.

(11) **James Miller**[8]—born in 1850; died 11 October,1917 at 66 years of age; unmarried.

(12) **Alice (Miller) (Hilton) Richardson**[8]—born in 1851; married 1st **Stephen Hilton** (son of Nathan) in 1870; and married 2nd **Charles B. Richardson** (son of Samuel & Lydia (Perry) Richardson). Alice died 19 September, 1895 at 44 years of age.*(see page 66)*

(13) **Elkanah Clements Miller**[8]—born in 1856; married **Mary Ella 'Nellie' Head** (daughter of Reuben & Lois Jane (Beardsley) Head) on 3 February, 1883. Nellie was born 3 October,1862 and died 12 November, 1916.

Isaac married second **Joanna Dukeshire** and they had 1 child:

(i) **Gertrude (Miller) (Sabeau)Crowell**[9]—married 1st **Willis Sabeau** and 2nd **Forman Crowell**.

DESCENDENTS OF SAMUEL JAMES PERRY
5th child of LEVI PERRY

SAMUEL JAMES PERRY[7]
son of: Levi[6], Moses[5], Samuel[4], Ezra[3], Ezra[2], Edmund[1]

BORN: 6 August, 1802 in Chebogue, Yarmouth Co. .
MARRIED: **Mary Margaret Brown** (daughter of Robert & Eunice (Doty) Brown) on 12 October, 1807 on Cape Sable Island, Nova Scotia by Asa MacGray. Mary was born 12 October, 1807 and died 28 October,1888.
DIED: predeceased Mary (1888).
CHILDREN: 1. **Eunice (Perry) Rapp**[8]—born in 10 July, 1834 in Barrington, N.S.; married **John Thomas Rapp** (a 36 year old widower) (son of James & Mary Rapp from McNutt's Island, Nova Scotia) on 6 July, 1875.

2. **Phoebe Ann (Perry)(Doane)Perry**[8]—born 3 Oct.1837; married 1st **Emery Doane** (son of William & Sophronia (Perry)Doane); 2nd married **John H. Perry** (age 46-widower from Black Point, Shelburne County, Nova Scotia) (son of Rufus & Belina Perry) on 27 December,1880.

3. **Levi Perry** [8]—born 22 December,1839; married 1st **Naomi Greenwood** (daughter of Hugh and Margaret (Rapp) Greenwood) from Cape Negro Island) on 15 January, 1864. Naomi died 6 July, 1866. Levi married 2nd **Catherine Ann Greenwood** (daughter of William and Mary Ann Greenwood) on 23 December, 1868.Levi was a fisherman.

4. **John B. Perry**[8]—born 11 May,1842; married **Lydia Perry** (age 27 years) (daughter of William and Margaret Perry from Red Head, Nova Scotia) on 7 December,1870. The marriage was performed by Rev. R.H. Taylor. John was a fisherman. John and Lydia had one daughter:
   (1) **Sarah (Perry) Atkinson**[9] –born 1873; married **Thomas M. Atkinson** of Stoney Island, Nova Scotia.

5. **Moses Perry**[8]—born in 1846; married **Cynthia Cook** (age 16 years) (daughter of John and Margaret (Littlewood) Cook) from Ingomar, Nova Scotia on 4 March, 1874.

6. **Barbara (Perry) Greenwood**[8]—born in 1848 or 1849; married **Lorenzo Greenwood** (son of Evan and Margaret Greenwood from Cape Negro Island).

LEVI PERRY[8]
son of :   Samuel[7], Levi[6], Moses[5], Samuel[4], Ezra[3], Ezra[2], Edmund[1]

BORN: 22 December, 1839.
MARRIED: 1st **Naomi Greenwood** (daughter of Hugh and Margaret Greenwood from Cape Sable Island) on 18 January,1864. Naomi died 6 July,1866, and Levi married 2nd **Catherine Ann Greenwood** (age 24) (daughter of William and Mary Ann Greenwood). Catherine and Levi were married by Rev .R. H. Taylor, Wesleyan Methodist Church. Catherine was born 17 November, 1844, and died 13 September, 1923 of pneumonia.
DIED: 30 April, 1912 of cancer. Both Levi and Catherine are buried on Cape Negro Island.
CHILDREN:(by Naomi)
          1. **Margaret A. (Perry)(Stalker) Snow**[9]—born 1864 or 1865; married 1st **John Stalker** (a widower) on 11 September, 1897; and 2nd married **Irving Snow** from Upper Port LeTour, Nova Scotia. There were no children from either marriage. Margaret is buried in the Municipal Plot, Brass Hill.
(by Catherine) 2. **Franklyn Leslie Perry**[9]—born 6 December, 1871 on Cape Negro Island; married 1st **Seretha Greenwood** (daughter of Ewen & Mehitable Greenwood from Cape Negro Island) on 26 February, 1895. Seretha died 4 March, 1897 at age 27 years. There were no children from this marriage. The 2nd marriage was to **Sadie Sarah Myrick** (daughter of Walter & Barbara Myrick from Blanche, Shelburne County, Nova Scotia) on 13 October, 1915. Franklyn Leslie died 14 December,1934. Franklyn and Sadie had 5 children:

(1) **Lloyd Franklin Perry**[10]—1st married **Gertrude Nickerson** and 2nd married **Amelia (Flemming) Crowell** (widow of Victor Crowell).

(2) **Gladys D. (Perry) Strang**[10]—married **Kenneth Strang.**

(3) **Leland Perry**[10]—married **Olive Grant.**

(4) **Bernice Isabel (Perry) Cross**[10]— married **Allan Cross.**

(5) **Ina (Perry) Hass**[10]—married **Eric Hass.**

3. **Samuel Albert Perry**[9]—born 27 September,1873; married and lived in Massachusetts and is buried there.

4. **Avery Dean Perry**[9]—born 9 November,1878; died 15 February, 1879 and is buried in Cape Negro Cemetery.

5. **Mary Bertha Perry**[9]—born 7 March, 1880; died 4 August,1892 and is buried on Cape Negro Island.

6. **Chester Woodman Perry**[9]—(twin of Ella Maywood)—born 20 October, 1883. Chester married **Cora Bell Goodwin** (daughter of William & Ada (Langthorne) Goodwin from Bear Point, Shelburne County, Nova Scotia). Chester died 19 June, 1956 and is buried in Atwood's Brook Cemetery in Shelburne County, Nova Scotia. Chester Woodman and Cora had 5 children:

(1) **Lena Viola (Perry)(Atkinson) Nickerson**[10] —born 22 Jan. 1912; married 1st **Ernest Atkinson** from Port Maitland, Nova Scotia. Married 2nd **Aubrey Nickerson** from Woods Harbour, Nova Scotia. Lena and Ernest had one child:

(i) **Muriel (Atkinson) Cottreau**[11]—married **Leonard Cottreau** on 31 July, 1965.

(2) **Avery Palmer Perry**[10]—born 8 February, 1914; married **Hazel Bower** from Jordan Falls, Nova Scotia. Avery died 24 December, 1978. Avery and Hazel had 6 children:

(i) **Terrance Perry**[11]—married **Shirley Ryer** from Barrington, Nova Scotia.

(ii) **Joseph Perry**[11]—married **Linda_?_.**

(iii) **Muriel (Perry) Young**[11]—married **Terrance Young** from Shelburne, Nova Scotia. Muriel and Terrance have since divorced.

(iv) **Wayne Perry**[11]—married **Lynne Freeman.**

(v) **Gordon Perry**[11]—married 1st **Ruth Hatfield**, 2nd **Jane Brown.**

(vi) **Raymond Perry**[11]

(3) **Mildred Ernesta (Perry) (Nickerson) Cummings**[10]—born 10 July,1918; married 1st **Fred H. Nickerson**; 2nd **Lloyd Cummings.** Mildred and Fred had 3 children:

(i) **Gloria Viola (Nickerson) Dube**[11]—married **Andre Dube** from Quebec.

(ii) **Howard Woodman Nickerson**[11]—married **Jean Decker** from Barrington, Nova Scotia.

(iii) **Avery Russell Nickerson**[11]—married **Lorna Adams** from Mahone Bay, Nova Scotia.

(4) **Ruth Armintha (Perry) Nickerson**[10]—born 7 December, 1915; married **Erdie Nickerson** of Doctor's Cove, Nova Scotia. Ruth and Erdie had 4 children:

    (i) **Richard Brian Nickerson**[11]—married **Mayola Larkin** from Woods Harbour, Nova Scotia.

    (ii) **Frank Melbourne Nickerson**[11]—married **Lillian Garron** from Forbes Point, Nova Scotia.

    (iii) **Sharon Elaine (Nickerson) Harris**[11]—married **Lloyd Harris** from Welchtown, Nova Scotia. Sharon and Lloyd have since divorced.

    (iv) **Roddy Michael Nickerson**[11]—married **Miss Colberson** of New Brunswick.

(5) **Herbert Leslie Perry**[10]—born 10 December, 1930; married **Isabel Snow** of Coffincroft, Nova Scotia; died 30 December, 1966. They had three children:

    (i) **Leslie Perry**[11]

    (ii) **Hope Perry**[11]

    (iii) **Phyllis Perry**[11]

7. **Ella Maywood Perry**[9]—(twin of Chester Woodman)— born 20 October, 1883. Ella died 3 October, 1893 and is buried on Cape Negro Island.

8. **Hanson Philbrooke Perry**[9]—born 1 March, 1886; married **Mary Osborne Kenney** (daughter of James A. and Jael Blanche (Downey) Kenney from Barrington West). Mary died 13 July,1949. Hanson died 27 December, 1937 of coronary thrombosis. Both Hanson and Mary are buried in Hillside Cemetery, Brass Hill, Shelburne County, Nova Scotia. Hanson Philbrooke and Mary had 5 children:

  (1) **Blanche Seretha (Perry) Baker**[10]—born 23 August, 1912; married **Enoch Vaughn Baker** on 14 November, 1959.

  (2) **Philbrooke Osborne Perry**[10]—born 29 June, 1914; married **Eugenie Faith Turner** (daughter of Anson from Manitoba) on 9 February, 1946. Philbrooke died 6 March, 1976, and is buried in Camp Hill Cemetery, Halifax Nova Scotia. Philbrooke and Eugenie had one son:

    (i) **Michael Hanson Perry**[11]—married **Thelma Kendall Grice** from Halifax on 17 December, 1977. Michael and Thelma had four children—two of whom were :

      (a) **May Perry**[12]

      (b) **Bahji Perry**[12]

  (3) **Albert William Perry**[10]—born 6 June, 1916; married **Hattie Alice Allen** (daughter of Imbert & Alice Allen from East Advocate, Nova Scotia),on 5 July, 1944. Albert William died 7 January,1995 and is buried in River Dale Cemetery in Barrington, Nova Scotia. Albert and Hattie had 2 children:

    (i) **Rachel Dorothy (Perry) Nickerson**[11] —born 19 October, 1955; married **Richard Clyde Nickerson** (son of Gary & Dellas (Smith) Nickerson of Barrington)

(ii) **Deborah Joy (Perry) Ward**[11]—married **Michael Peter Ward** (the son of Peter from Vernon, British Columbia) on 15 August, 1980.

Albert William's obituary read:

PERRY, Albert William—78, at Barrington, Shelburne Co., died January 7, 1995 at home. Born in Barrington, he was a son of the late Hanson P. and Mary O. (Kenney) Perry. He was a veteran of the Second World War, serving in active service for five years. He was a founding member of Barrington 7-E Fire Department and a certified electrician for many years. Surviving are his wife, the former Hattie Allen; daughters, Rachel (Mrs. Richard Nickerson), Barrington; Deborah (Mrs. Michael Ward) Vancouver, B.C.; brother, James, Crowell's Post Office; sister, Blanche (Mrs. Vaughn Baker), Dartmouth. He was predeceased by a brother, Philbrooke; sister, Catherine. Visitation will be 2-4, 7-9 p.m. today in H. Huskilson's Funeral Home, Barrington. Procession leaving funeral home 2 p.m. Tuesday for cemetery for graveside service. Rev. Everette Nickerson officiating.

(4) **Catherine Elizabeth Perry**[10]—born 2 October,1918; died 2 April, 1941. She is buried in Hillside Cemetery, Brass Hill, Shelburne County, Nova Scotia.

(5) **James Levi Perry**[10]—born 17 July,1920; married **Ruth Elaine Lyons** (daughter of Dennis from Barrington Passage) on 1 September, 1941. James and Ruth had 2 children:

(i) **Marianne Elaine (Perry) (Byrne) Sears**[11]—married 1st **Robert Byrne** on 5 December, 1981(divorced) ; 2nd **Gregory Sears** of Shag Harbour, N.S.

(ii) **Rosalie Joyce (Perry) McMullin**[11]—married **Stephen McMullin** from New Brunswick on 5 July, 1980. They had two children:

(a) **Nancy Ruth McMullin**[12]

(b) **Kevin James McMullin**[12]

9. **Wilfred Ernest Perry**[9]—born 14 July, 1877; married **Ida Frances Swaine** (daughter of Paul & Elizabeth Swaine from Blanche, Shelburne County, Nova Scotia) on 25 February, 1899; died 17 June, 1933 of cancer. After Wilfred died, Ida married **Walter Myrick**. Ida and Walter had no children. Ida died 14 August,1972. Wilfred and Ida had 2 children:

(1) **Ella Maywood (Perry) Thomas**[10]—married **Harmond Thomas** from Blanche, Shelburne County, N.S. They moved to the U.S.A.

(2) **Ileta Annie (Perry) Thomas**[10]—married **John Wilbert Thomas** (son of George Thomas). Ileta and John had a daughter:

(i) **Lola (Thomas) O'Connell**[11] who married **Whitworth O'Connell** of Baccaro, Shelburne County, Nova Scotia.

MOSES PERRY[8]

son of: Samuel[7], Levi[6], Moses[5], Samuel[4], Ezra[3], Ezra[2], Edmund[1.]

BORN: 25 Jan. 1846 on Cape Sable Island.

MARRIED: **Cynthia Jane Cook** (daughter of John and Margaret (Littlewood) Cook) on 4 March, 1874. Cynthia was born 1 January 1859 in Chebogue, Yarmouth County and died 21 April, 1934 in Shag Harbour, Shelburne County.

The Cook family came to Yarmouth from Kingston, Massachusetts. Their ancestor, Francis Cook, came over on the "Mayflower". Cynthia married Moses Perry in 1874 when she was 15 years old, and bore him 10 children. After Moses' death she married Ransome Langthorne.
        – from the New England Genealogy Register

DIED: circa 1905

CHILDREN:

1. **Delilah Perry[9]**—born 1876; died 1 November, 1882.
2. **Frederick Manasseh Clinton Perry[9]**—born 14 February,1881; married **Ina Ethel Cook** (30 July, 1890—22 April, 1969) on 30 October, 1907.
3. **Edwin 'Eddie' Perry[9]**— moved to Newfoundland and did not keep in touch with the family.
4. **Eldridge "Ellie" Perry[9]**—born 1890; married **Esther (Reed) Huskins** from Clam Point, Nova Scotia; died 20 December, 1936.
5. **Delcina (Perry) Rodgerson[9]**—married **John Henry Rodgerson** (from Yarmouth, Nova Scotia) on 27 April, 1904 at Shag Harbour, Nova Scotia.
6. **Matilda (Perry) Nickerson[9]**—born 15 December,1888; married **Freeland Nickerson** (widower) (1880-1931) in 1909. Freeland's first marriage was to **Althea Ann Penney**. Matilda died in October,1956.
7. **Frances (Perry) Saulnier[9]**—born at Cape Negro in 1894; married **Howard Saulnier**, and she died in 1936.
8. **Ida (Perry) Nickerson[9]**—born in 1897; married **Locksley Nickerson** (from Shag Harbour, Nova Scotia) and Ida died in 1965.
9. **Sanford Perry[9]**—died in his teens and is buried on Cape Negro Island, Nova Scotia.
10. **Clarence Perry[9]**—born 5 March, 1897; drowned 12 March, 1912, 2 miles off of Jordan Bay, Nova Scotia on the Glouchester schooner *"Patrician".(see Lost Mariners of Shelburne County, Vol.1)*

"In 1904 or 1905, Moses Perry's house burnt down and the family moved off of Cape Negro Island"
        - from Cape Negro Island by Pearl McCoy

FREDERICK MANASSEH CLINTON PERRY[9]

son of: Moses[8], Samuel[7], Levi[6], Moses[5], Samuel[4], Ezra[3], Ezra[2], Edmund[1].

BORN: 14 February, 1881 on Cape Negro Island.

MARRIED: **Ina Ethel Cook** (1890-1969) (daughter of George and Annie (Nickerson) Cook) on 30 October, 1907.

DIED: November 1954 in Shag Harbour, N.S. Both Fred and Ina are buried in the Bear Point Cemetery.

CHILDREN : 1. **Dora Evangeline (Perry) Smith**[10]—born 30 Dec. 1908; married **Herman 'Leland' Smith** on 6 April, 1929; died 28 February, 1935.

            2. **Winnifred Ethel (Perry) Nickerson**[10]—born 16 October, 1910; married **Sidney Nickerson** on 13 September, 1931; died 23 June, 1989.

            3. **Jean Viola (Perry) Corning**[10]—born 1 May 1912; died 15 Nov. 1992; married **Harold Arthur Corning** (1908-1983) (son of Albert & Daisy (Lawrence) Corning) on 11 July, 1930.

            4. **Gladys Cook (Perry) Palmer**[10]—born 23 Nov.1914; married **Raymond Chelsey Palmer** (12 April, 1904—11 April, 1983) on 10 November, 1934.

            5. **Annie Althea (Perry) Smith**[10]—born 1 September, 1916; married **Leslie Stanford Smith** in 1935 Althea died 10 of May 2011.

            6. **George Fred Perry (Rev.)**[10]—married **Edith Greenwood** on 31 December, 1939.

            7. **Charlotte Maude (Perry) Smith**[10]—born 4 March, 1925; married **Maynard Smith** (7 February, 1920—24 September, 1978) on 28 July, 1948. Charlotte died 15 May 2011.

            8. **Margaret Veda (Perry) Cameron**[10]—married **John Cameron** on 15 June, 1949.

            9. **Leslie Wayne Perry**[10]—born 2 July, 1944 (adopted); married **Heather Brannen** on 14 August, 1965. Wayne died 31 August, 1986.

DORA EVANGELINE (PERRY) SMITH[10]

daughter of : Frederick[9], Moses[8], Samuel[7], Levi[6], Moses[5], Samuel[4], Ezra[3], Ezra[2], Edmund[1].

BORN: 30 December, 1908; Bear Point, Shelburne Co.

MARRIED: **Herman Leland Smith** (3 May, 1901- 9 Sept.1962) on 6 April, 1927.

DIED: 28 February, 1935 of meningitis.

CHILDREN: 1. **Ella Maude (Smith) Richards**[11] (twin of Ethel Mildred)—born 29 January, 1930. Ella married **Erwin Leslie Richards** on 3 July, 1954. Ella died 30 April, 2013. They had 2 children:

          (1) **Elizabeth Ann (Richards) Burdock**[12]—married **John Burdock** on 30 August, 1980. Elizabeth Ann and John have 3 children:

             (i) **Tracey Joanne Burdock**[13]

             (ii) **Sean Allen Burdock**[13]—(twin of John Evan)

(iii) **John Evan Burdock**[13]—(twin of Sean Allen)
(2) **Stephen Erwin Richards**[12]
2. **Ethel Mildred (Smith) Richards**[11] (twin of Ella)— Ethel married **Melbourne Sinclair Richards** (brother of Erwin) on 2 January,1958. Ethel and Sinclair had 2 children:
(1). **Kathryn Jean (Richards) Kirby**[12]—married **David Christopher Kirby** on 9 August, 1992. Kathryn and David have a son:
(i) **Christopher Frederick Kirby**[13]
(2) **Susan Lee Richards**[12].

WINNIFRED ETHEL (PERRY) NICKERSON[10]
daughter of : Frederick[9], Moses[8], Samuel[7], Levi[6], Moses[5], Samuel[4], Ezra[3], Ezra[2], Edmund[1].

BORN: 16 October, 1910 at Bear Point, Shelburne County, Nova Scotia.
MARRIED: **Sidney Nickerson** on 13 September, 1931.
DIED: 23 June, 1989 in Halifax, Nova Scotia of cancer. Buried in Doctor's Cove.
CHILDREN: 1. **Vera (Nickerson) Garron**[11]-married **Morton Garron** .Vera and Morton had:
(1) **Jerry Lee (Garron) Atwood**[12]—married **Stephen Atwood**. Jerry Lee and Stephen had 2 children:
(i) **Davis Atwood**[13]
(ii) **Darcy Atwood**[13]
(2) **Sherry (Garron) Smith**[12]—married **Paul Smith** on 22 June, 1974. Sherry and Paul had 3 children:
(i) **Stacy Smith**[13]
(ii) **Morton Smith**[13]
(iii) **Samantha Smith**[13]
(3) **Kensley Garron**[12]
2. **Sidney Rupert 'Bubby' Nickerson**[11]—born at Atwood's Brook, Shelburne County, Nova Scotia; married **Helen Pothier** on 30 June, 1954. Sidney and Helen had:
(1) **Dale Nickerson**[12]
(2) **Donna (Nickerson) d'Entremont**[12] - married **Howard d'Entremont** on 10 November, 1984. Donna and Howard had 3 children:
(i) **Matthew d'Entremont**[13]
(ii) **Sarah d'Entremont**[13]
(iii) **Erica d'Entremont**[13]

JEAN VIOLA (PERRY) CORNING[10]
daughter of : Frederick[9], Moses[8], Samuel[7], Levi[6], Moses[5], Samuel[4], Ezra[3], Ezra[2], Edmund[1].

BORN: 1 May, 1912 at Bear Point, Shelburne County, Nova Scotia.
MARRIED: **Harold Arthur Corning** (7 January, 1908-13 January, 1983)(son of Albert and Daisy (Lawrence) Corning from Yarmouth, Nova Scotia) on 11 July, 1930.

DIED:	15 November, 1992 at Yarmouth Hospital.
CHILDREN:	1. **Blanche Jean (Corning) Firth**[11]—born 29 July, 1931; died 1 September, 2011; married **Bernard Eugene Firth** (son of Harry and Reta (Decker) Firth) from Sandy Point, Shelburne County, Nova Scotia) on 5 June, 1954. Blanche and Bernie were married at the Zion Baptist Church in Yarmouth.
	2. **Mary Ann (Corning) Mitchell**[11]—born in Yarmouth, Nova Scotia; married **Dr. Theodore 'Ted' John Mitchell** (son of Margaret (Lonsberry) (Mitchell) Church and Theodore Earle Mitchell) from Calgary, Alberta on 4 September,1965. Mary Ann and Ted were married at the Zion Baptist Church in Yarmouth. Mary Ann and Ted had 2 children:
	(1) **Theodore Arthur Mitchell**[12]—born in Ottawa, Ontario.-partner **Deborah Textor** (daughter of Charlotte (Lowery) and David Textor) from California/Arkansas.
	(2) **Shawn Patrick Mitchell**[12]—born in Ottawa, Ontario. Shawn married **Tricia Anne Bolyard** (daughter of Tim and Kim (Alderson) Bolyard) from Oberammergau, Germany on August 16, 2010 at Lake Tahoe, Nevada.
	The Mitchells moved to Reno, Nevada in 1985.

BLANCHE JEAN (CORNING) FIRTH[11]

daughter of :   Jean (Perry) Corning[10], Frederick[9], Moses[8], Samuel[7], Levi[6], Moses[5], Samuel[4], Ezra[3], Ezra[2], Edmund[1].

BORN:	29 July, 1931
MARRIED:	**Bernard Eugene Firth** (son of Harry and Reta (Decker) Firth from Sandy Point, Nova Scotia) on 5 June, 1954.
DIED:	1 Sept. 2011
CHILDREN:	1. **Heather Jean (Firth) McClelland**[12]—married **Michael Bruce McClelland** (son of John and Helen (Lynn) McClelland from Truro, Nova Scotia, formerly from Ireland) on 27 August, 1977. Heather and Michael had 2 children:
	(1) **Patrick Michael McClelland**[13]—Married **Mindy Wellband** and they had:
	(i) **Cameron James McClelland**[14]-born in Halifax, Nova Scotia.
	(2) **Jennifer Jean McClelland**[13]
	2. **Holly Ann Reta (Firth) Cottreau**[12]—married **David Ambrose Cottreau** (son of Eva J. (Robinson) and Eugene Cottreau) from Yarmouth, Nova Scotia) .Holly and David had 2 sons:
	(1) **Matthew Eugene Cottreau**[13]—Married **Melissa Blondin** from Cape Breton Island on 22 Aug. 2009
	(2) **Jonathan Robert Cottreau**[13]—Married **Caitlin Regen** on 2 July 2011. Caitlin is the daughter of Hon. Geoff and Kelly Regan.
	3. **Mark Arthur Bernard Firth**[12]—married **Barbara Ruth Higby** (adopted daughter of Ann (Brown) and Alan Higby) from Port Maitland, Nova Scotia on 14 February, 1990.

4. **Heidie Dawn(Firth)(Midgley) Halliday**[12]-married **1st Paul Edward Midgley** (son of Ann (Whittaker) (Midgley) Davies and Bruce Midgley from Newton-la-Willows, England) on 17 November, 1990. Later divorced and Heidie married **Dale Halliday** on 22 October, 2008

GLADYS COOK (PERRY) PALMER[10]
daughter of : Frederick[9], Moses[8], Samuel[7], Levi[6], Moses[5], Samuel[4], Ezra[3], Ezra[2], Edmund[1].

BORN: 23 November, 1914 in Bear Point, Shelburne Co., N.S.
MARRIED: **Raymond Chelsey Palmer** (1904-1983) on 10 November, 1934.
DIED: 24 October, 2005 in Uxbridge, Massachusetts
CHILDREN: 1. **Frederick R. Palmer**[11]—married **Frances L. Shimkus** on 21 February, 1964. Frederick and Frances had three children:
            (1) **Frederick R. Palmer**[12]
            (2) **Faye L. Palmer**[12]
            (3) **Francine L. Palmer**[12]
         2. **Beatrice E. (Palmer) Burgess**[11]—married **Ellis M. Burgess** on 30 November, 1957. Beatrice and Ellis had 11 children.
         3. **Joyce (Palmer) Britt**[11]—married **James R. Britt** on 20 April, 1963. Joyce and James had 7 children.

BEATRICE (PALMER) BURGESS[11]
daughter of :   Gladys (Perry) Palmer[10], Frederick[9], Moses[8], Samuel[7], Levi[6], Moses[5], Samuel[4], Ezra[3], Ezra[2], Edmund[1].

MARRIED: **Ellis Burgess** on 30 November, 1957.
CHILDREN: 1. **Debra A. (Burgess) Grazulis**[12]—married **Robert D. Grazulis** on 26 June,1976. Debra and Robert had three children:
            (1) **David Grazulis**[13]
            (2) **Andrew Grazulis**[13]
            (3) **Rachael Grazulis**[13]
         2. **Ellis Burgess**[12]—married **Laura J. Steele** on 24 September, 1960. Ellis and Laura had two children:
            (1) **Justine Burgess**[13]
            (2) **Patrick Burgess**[13]
         3. **Jeffrey R. Burgess**[12]—married **Kim M. Corey** on 7 September, 1985. Jeffrey and Kim had one child:
            (1) **Holly A. Burgess**[13]
         4. **Donna L. Burgess**[12] -(twin of Darlene)
         5. **Darlene Joyce (Burgess) Dillion**[12] –(twin of Donna). Darlene married **John P. Dillion, Jr.**, on 4 May, 1991. Darlene and John had:
            (1) **Matthew John Dillion**[13]
         6. **Brian E. Burgess**[12]— (adopted). Brian had two children:
            (1) **Brittany S. Dow**[13]
            (2) **Bradley John Dow**[13]
         7. **Crystal J. (Burgess) Hipkins**[12]—married **Robert Hipkins, Jr.**, on 25 August, 1987.

8. **Nicholas D. Burgess**[12]— (adopted); married **Penelope Graves** on 18 November, 1989.
9. **Michael J. Burgess**[12]— (adopted).
10. **Scott A. Burgess**[12].
11.**Timothy J. Burgess**[12]— (adopted).

JOYCE I. (PALMER) BRITT[11]

daughter of :   Gladys (Perry) Palmer[10], Frederick[9], Moses[8], Samuel[7], Levi[6], Moses[5], Samuel[4], Ezra[3], Ezra[2], Edmund[1].

BORN: in Massachusetts
MARRIED: **James R. Britt** on 20 April,1963.
CHILDREN: 1. **Janet L. (Britt) Swart**[12]—married **Michael Swart** on 24 March, 1990.
  2. **Jean A. (Britt) (Feeley) Scocos**[12]—married 1st **Michael J. Feeley** . Jean and Michael had two children:
    (1) **Michael J. Feeley II**[13]
    (2) **Justine N. Feeley**[13]
       Jean and Michael were divorced and Jean married 2nd **Thomas Scocos**. Jean and Thomas had one child:
    (3) **Alexis R. Scocos**[13].
  3. **Daniel J. Britt**[12]— (adopted).
  4. **Thomas R. Britt**[12] (adopted).
  5. **Sharon J. Britt**[12]- (adopted).
  6. **Tammy J. Britt**[12]— (adopted).
  7. **James R. Britt** [12]— (adopted).

ANNIE ALTHEA (PERRY) SMITH[10]

daughter of :   Frederick[9], Moses[8], Samuel[7], Levi[6], Moses[5], Samuel[4], Ezra[3], Ezra[2], Edmund[1].
BORN: 1 September, 1916.
MARRIED: **Leslie Stanford Smith** (born 1913) in 1935. Les died in 2005.
DIED: 10 May, 2011 in Shelburne, Nova Scotia
CHILDREN: 1. **Morton Leslie Smith**[11]—married **Irene Elaine Smith** in 1965. Morton and Nancy had 2 children:
    (1) **Nancy Louise (Smith) Jones**[12]— married **Phillip Jones**. Nancy and Phillip had three children:

Althea and Les

    (i) **Laura Elizabeth Jones**[13]
    (ii) **Melissa Paige Jones**[13]
    (iii) **Phillip Thaine Jones**[13]
    (2) **Dennis Morton Smith**[12]-Married **Christine**.
  2. **Emery Douglas Smith**[11] —married **Hazel Amanda Smith** in 1957. Emery and Hazel had 2 children:
    (1) **Monty Emery Smith**[12]—married **Sharon Maxwell** in 1981. Monty and Sharon had three children:

(i) **Jeremy Andrew Smith**[13]—married **Kara MacKenzie**
    (ii) **Travis Leslie Douglas Smith**[13]—married **Debbie**
    (iii) **Shannon Monty Smith**[13]
  (2) **Joy Gail (Smith) Goreham**[12]—married **Michael Goreham.** Joy and Michael had two children:
    (i) **Jenna Michelle Goreham**[13]—married **Shaun Kennedy**
    (ii) **Brennan Curtis Douglas Goreham**[13]

GEORGE FRED PERRY (REV.) [10]

son of: Frederick[9], Moses[8], Samuel[7], Levi[6], Moses[5], Samuel[4], Ezra[3], Ezra[2], Edmund[1].

BORN: 3 September, 1918.
MARRIED: **Edith Lucille Joyce Greenwood** (born 6 March, 1918) on 31 Dec. 1938. Edith died 13 Feb. 2002 and is buried in Bear Point Cemetery.
CHILDREN: 1. **Jackie George Perry**[11]— 5 June, 1939 at Bear Point, Shelburne County, Nova Scotia. Jackie married 1st **Gail Bownes** on 3 April, 1959 at Chelsea, Maine. Jackie and Gail were divorced and he married 2nd **Lily** ?. Jackie died in 2005 in Kansas. Jackie and Gail had 3 children:
    (1) **Dana Carol Perry**[12]—born at Augusta, Maine.
    (2) **Tanya Lynn Perry**[12]—born at Fort Benning, Georgia.
    (3) **Penelope Alice Perry**[12]—born in Germany.
    2. **Rodney Clinton Perry**[11]—born at Bear Point, Shelburne County, Nova Scotia. Rodney married **Sharon Gail Clark** on 12 October, 1963 at Newark, New York. Rodney and Sharon have since divorced and he married **Marsha**. Rodney is still living in New York State. Rodney and Sharon had 4 children:
    (1) **Tammie Lee (Perry) Keagle**[12]—born at Newark, New York; married **Matthew Wayne Keagle**. Tammie Lee and Matthew had 3 children:
      (i) **Jennifer Lynn Keagle**[13]—born at New York.
      (ii) **Stephanie M. Keagle**[13] and **Michelle Lee Keagle**[13] **(twins)**—born at New York.
    (2) **Todd Christopher Perry**[12]—married **Laura Lynn Givien.**
    (3) **Leigh Ann Perry**[12]—born in Newark, New York.
    (4) **Rodney Clinton Perry**[12]—born in Newark, New York.
    3. **Gary Marshall Perry**[11]—married 1st **Signe Wheller** on 21 April, 1960 at Manchester, Maine. Gary and Signe were divorced and he married 2nd **Carrie.** Gary is currently living in Florida. Gary and Signe had 2 children:
    (1) **Robin Leslie Perry**[12]—born at Augusta, Maine. Robin had two children:
      (i) **Jamica**[13]
      (ii) **Joshua**[13]
    (2) **Craig Marshall Perry**[12]—born at Augusta, Maine.
    4. **Eric Thomas Perry**[11]—born at Bear Point, Shelburne County, Nova Scotia. He married **Alice Louise McPherson** of Hallowell, Maine, on

21 June 1962 at Hallowell, Maine. Eric is currently living in Augusta Maine.

Eric and Alice had 4 children:

  (1) **Eric James Perry**[12]—born at Augusta, Maine; married **Pamela Elaine Young** on 26 August, 1989 at Hallowell, Maine.

  (2) **John Harold Perry**[12]—born at Augusta, Maine.

  (3) **Daniel McPherson Perry**[12]-born at Augusta, Maine

  (4) **Jane Alice Perry**[12]—born at Augusta, Maine

5. **Dora Maxine (Perry)(Lyons) Breland**[11]—married 1st **Joseph Leigh Lyons, Sr.** at Smoaks, South Carolina. She married 2nd **William Preston Breland Jr.** on 20 January,1990 at Smoaks, South Carolina. Dora and Joseph had 3 children:

  (1) **Maxine Victoria (Lyons) Prater**[12]—born at Waterloo, South Carolina; married **Alvin Emerson Prater** in South Carolina. Maxine and Alvin had 2 children:

    (i) **Elizabeth Nicole Prater**[13]—born at Waterloo, South Carolina

    (ii) a daughter-born at Waterloo, South Carolina. married **Larry Michael Stowe** on 21 April, 1990 at Waterloo, South Carolina.

  (2) **Joseph Leigh Lyons**[12]—born at Orangeburg, South Carolina.

  (3) **Joy Ann Lyons**[12]—born at Waterloo, South Carolina.

In July 1995, Rev. George preached for his family and friends at the Bear Point Church

CHARLOTTE MAUDE (PERRY) SMITH[10]

daughter of :   Frederick[9], Moses[8], Samuel[7], Levi[6], Moses[5], Samuel[4], Ezra[3], Ezra[2], Edmund[1.]

BORN: 4 March, 1925 in Bear Point, Shelb. Co.

MARRIED: **Maynard Wentworth Smith** (born 7 February, 1920-died 24 Sept.,1978) on 28 July, 1948.

DIED: 15 May, 2011 in Shelburne, Nova Scotia

CHILDREN: 1. **Donna Charlotte (Smith) Dexter**[11]

—married **Michael Dexter** on 24 February, 1968. Donna and Michael had 4 children:

  (1) **Angela Lynn Dexter**[12]-has 1 son (i) **Spenser Michael**[13]

  (2) **Traci (Dexter) Nickerson**[12]—married **Charles Nickerson** on 17 October, 1992.Traci has 5 children:

    (i) **Danielle Nickerson**[13]married **Hailie Jayne** on 24 Jan. 2008

    (ii) **Kayla Nicholle Nickerson**[13]

    (iii) **Kassidy Shae-Lynn Nickerson**[13]

    (iv) **Kiara Lee Nickerson**[13]

    (v) **Brady McKay Nickerson**[13].

  (3) **Gillian (Dexter) Reynolds**[12]—married **Joey Alex Clarke Reynolds** on 25 Feb. 1995. They had:

    (a) **Kayden Alexander Reynolds**[13]

(4) **Kristen Noel Dexter**[12]—married **Lorie Colleen Nickerson** on 18 April, 2000. They have :

(a) **Jerid Kristin Dexter**[13]

Charlotte worked at the Shelburne Furniture Store for 28 years; she was past president of the Kinettes, a life time member of the Roseway Hospital Auxillary, and a Brownie leader

------------ *Thanks to Donna (Smith) Dexter*

MARGARET VEDA (PERRY) CAMERON[10]

daughter of : Frederick[9], Moses[8], Samuel[7], Levi[6], Moses[5], Samuel[4], Ezra[3], Ezra[2], Edmund[1].

MARRIED: **John Cameron** on 15 June,1949 at Bear Point, Nova Scotia.

CHILDREN: 1. **Scott John Cameron**[11]—born in Yarmouth, Nova Scotia; married **Lea Ann April Harding** (daughter of Mrs. Ernest O'Connell and the late Arthur Forbes). Scott and Lea Ann had a daughter:

(1) **Farryn Samantha Rose Cameron**[12]

LESLIE WAYNE PERRY[10]

son of : Frederick[9], Moses[8], Samuel[7], Levi[6], Moses[5], Samuel[4], Ezra[3], Ezra[2], Edmund[1].

BORN: 2 July, 1944 (adopted)

MARRIED: **Heather Brannen** on 14 August, 1965.

DIED: 1986 in an automobile accident, and is buried in Bear Point Cemetery.

CHILDREN: 1. **Christopher Perry**[11]—married **Lesa O'Connell** on 22 November, 1990. Christopher and Lesa had 2 sons :

(1) **Garrett Wayne Perry**[12]

(2) **Dalton Christopher Perry**[12]

2. **Timothy Perry**[11]

3. **David Aaron Perry**[11]

4. **Matthew Perry**[11]

5. **Faith Marinda Ann Perry**[11]

DELCINA VINGENETTA (PERRY) RODGERSON[9]

daughter of: Moses[8], Samuel[7], Levi[6], Moses[5], Samuel[4], Ezra[3], Ezra[2], Edmund[1].

MARRIED: **John Henry Rodgerson** (born 19 August, 1861) from Yarmouth on 27 April, 1904 at Shag Harbour, Nova Scotia.

CHILDREN: 1. **Oren Burton Rodgerson**[10]—believed to have died in a Toronto hospital of war injuries.

2. **Elizabeth Ann Rodgerson**[10].

3. **Helen Esther Rodgerson**[10]—married and moved to California. Helen Esther died in 1992.

4. **Sanford Eugene Rodgerson**[10]—baptized **James Sanford** and is known by his family by this name; married **Madeline Feener**. James and Madeline had two children:

      (1) **Marilyn (Rodgerson) Comeau**[11]—married **Ken Comeau** and they had:
         (i) **Terry Comeau**[12] —who has two children
         (ii) **Erin Comeau**[12]
      (2) **Joyce Rodgerson**[11]—adopted.

5. <u>**John Alvin Rodgerson**</u>[10]—married **Ida Harding**. John was lost at sea 13 July, 1967.
6. <u>**Ralph LeRoy Rodgerson**</u>[10] (twin of Russell Clifton)—born 13 February, 1916; married **Marion Ethel Harding.**
7. <u>**Russell Clifton Rodgerson**</u>[10] (twin of Ralph LeRoy)—born 13 February, 1916; baptized **James Russell** and was known by his family by this name; married **Mary Celeste LeBlanc.** James Russell died 13 May, 1980.
8. <u>**Mary Edna (Rodgerson) (Harding) Cook**</u>[10]—married 1st **Leland Harding** and 2nd **Victor Cook.**
9. <u>**Phyllis Bernice (Rodgerson)(Haley) Chandler**</u>[10]—married 1st **William Haley,** and 2nd **Mr.Chandler.**

JOHN ALVIN RODGERSON[10]

  son of: Delcina (Perry) Rodgerson[9], Moses[8], Samuel[7], Levi[6], Moses[5], Samuel[4], Ezra[3], Ezra[2], Edmund[1].

MARRIED: **Ida Harding**
DIED: 13 July, 1967. Lost at sea.
CHILDREN: 1. **Carolyn (Rodgerson) Muise**[11]— married **Raymond Muise** and had:
      (1) **Kevin Muise**[12] who is married and had two children:
       (i) **Jeffery Muise**[13]
       (ii) **Jennifer Muise**[13].
    2. **Joan (Rodgerson) d'Entremont**[11]—married **Jules d'Entremont** and they had:
      (1) **Craig d'Entremont**[12]
      (2) **Charlene d'Entremont**[12]
      (3) **Vaughn d'Entremont**[12]
      (4) **April d'Entremont**[12]
    3. **Lorraine (Rodgerson) (Muise) Boudreau**[11] —married 1st **'Buddy' Muise** and 2nd **Abel Boudreau.** Lorraine had:
      (1) **Judy Rodgerson**[12]
      (2) **John Rodgerson**[12]
      (3) **Michael Muise**[12]
    4. **Alvin Rodgerson**[11] —married 1st **Adra Smith** and 2nd **Dorothy Rogers.** Alvin and Adra had:
      (1) **Tammy Rodgerson**[12]
      (2) **Randy Rodgerson**[12]
      (3) **Brian Rodgerson**[12]
      (4) **Blaine Rodgerson**[12]
      (5) **Terry Rodgerson**[12]
      (6) **Kenny Rodgerson**[12]

Alvin and Dorothy had:
(7) **Chrissie Rodgerson**[12]

RALPH LEROY RODGERSON[10]

son of: Delcina (Perry) Rodgerson[9], Moses[8], Samuel[7], Levi[6], Moses[5], Samuel[4], Ezra[3], Ezra[2], Edmund[1].

BORN: 15 February, 1917 (twin of Russell Clifton)
MARRIED: **Ethel Marion Harding**—born 23 June, 1918
DIED: 17 March, 1976
CHILDREN: 1. **Nellie Vingenetta (Rodgerson) (Comeau)Marshall**[11]—Nellie married 1st **Richard B. Comeau** and 2nd **Frank Marshall.** Nellie and Richard Comeau had four children:
 (1) **Susan Yvonne (Comeau) (Higby) Muise**[12]—Susan married 1st **John Higby** (deceased), and 2nd **Mike Muise.** Susan and John Higby had a daughter:
  (i) **Samantha Sue Higby**[13]
A second daughter of Susan's was later adopted by her second husband:
  (ii) **Ashley Nicole Muise**[13].
 (2) **Richard Comeau**[12]
 (3) **Joyce Marion Comeau**[12]—Joyce Marion had one child:
  (i) **Jamie Richard Comeau**[13]
 (4) **Dana Louise (Marshall) Smith**[12]—(Dana Louise was adopted by Frank). She married **Todd Smith.**
  2. **LeRoy Ralph Rodgerson**[11]—married **Andrea Nickerson** and they had:
 (1) **Troy Lee William Rodgerson**[12]—Troy married **Heather Murphy** and they had two children:
  (i) **Jordon Troy Rodgerson**[13]
  (ii) **Lance Kenneth LeRoy Rodgerson**[13]
 (2) **Sherry Anne (Rodgerson) Anthony**[12]—married **Robert Anthony.** Sherry and Robert had one child:
  (i) **Holly Christina Anthony**[13]
  3. **Pamela Lee (Rodgerson) Pothier**[11]—married **Raymond W. Pothier** and they had:
 (1) **Amber Dawn Pothier**[12].
 (2) **Brett William Pothier**[12]
 (3) **Shelby Dawn Pothier**[12]

RUSSELL CLIFTON RODGERSON[10]

son of: Delcina (Perry) Rodgerson[9], Moses[8], Samuel[7], Levi[6], Moses[5], Samuel[4], Ezra[3], Ezra[2], Edmund[1].

BORN: 13 February, 1916 (twin of Ralph LeRoy)
MARRIED   **Mary Celeste LeBlanc.** Russell was baptized James Russell.
DIED: 13 May , 1980.
CHILDREN: 1. **Cecil Rodgerson**[11]—died at birth.

2. **James Robert Rodgerson**[11]—born 28 April, 1936; married **Yvonne Doucette** and they had:
   (1) **Constance Elaine (Rodgerson) Nickerson**[12] —adopted. Constance married **Michael Nickerson** and they had:
      (i) **Crystal Nickerson**[13]
      (ii) **Justin Nickerson**[13]
   (2) **Theresa Darlene(Rodgerson) Dulong**[12] —adopted. Theresa had:
      (i) **Tyler Louis Rodgerson**[13]
      Theresa Darlene married **James Dulong.**
3. **George Russell Rodgerson**[11]—married **Mary Pauline Saulnier** and they had:
   (1) **Curtis Russell Rodgerson**[12]—married **Louise Rose Hawerychuk** on 17 September, 1988 and they had:
      (i) **Curtis Nicholas Rodgerson**[13]
      (ii) **Alex Rodgerson**[13].
   (2) **Elaine Anne (Rodgerson) Jubis**[12]—married **Michael David Jubis** on 2 September, 1989, and they had:
      (i) **Michael Ryan Jubis**[13]
      (ii) **Christian Jubis**[13].
   3) **Wanda Marie (Rodgerson) Deveau**[12] —married **Mark Daniel Deveau** on 21 August, 1993.
4. **Paul Rodgerson**[11]—died at birth.
5. **William Stuart Rodgerson**[11]—married **Betty Ann Surette** and had:
   (1) **Stuart Rodgerson**[12].
6. **David Rodgerson**[11]—died at approximately 3 years of age from polio.
7. **Joseph David 'Midge' Rodgerson**[11]—married 1st **Sharron Doucette** and 2nd **Marie Pauline Surette.** Sharron and Joseph had:
   (1) **Shelley Marie Rodgerson**[12]—Shelley had two children
      (i) **Marc Eric Rodgerson**[13]
      (ii) **Holly Marie Rodgerson**[13]
8. **Donald Bruce Rodgerson**[11]—married 1st **Faye Thomas** and 2nd **Nancy Watters.** Donald and Faye had:
   (1) **Kelly Rodgerson**[12]
   (2) **Melissa Rodgerson**[12].
      Donald and Nancy had:
   (3) **Alexandra 'Sandy' Rodgerson**[12]
9. **Sharon Ann (Rodgerson) MacDonald**[11] —married **Paul MacDonald** and they had:
   (1) **Paul MacDonald**[12]
   (2) **Lori MacDonald**[12] who has a daughter :
      (i) **Katie MacDonald**[13]
10. **John Brian Rodgerson**[11]—married 1st **Roselyn Humber** and 2nd **Cheryl Turner**. John Brian and Roselyn had:
    (1) **Carrie Rodgerson**[12]
    (2) **Cory Rodgerson**[12]
11. **Judith Ann Linda (Rodgerson) Walters**[11] —married **Gregory N. Walters** and they had:
    (1) **Gregory Walters**[12]
    (2) **Justin Walters**[12]

MARY EDNA (RODGERSON) HARDING, COOK[10]

daughter of: Delcina (Perry) Rodgerson[9], Moses[8], Samuel[7], Levi[6], Moses[5], Samuel[4], Ezra[3], Ezra[2], Edmund[1].

MARRIED: 1st **Leland Harding** and 2nd **Victor Cook.**
CHILDREN: (by Leland)

1. **Shirley (Harding) Hanf**[11]—married **Prescott Hanf** and they had:
(1) **Judy (Hanf) LeBlanc**[12]— married **Brian LeBlanc** and they had:
(i) **Quinton LeBlanc**[13]. Quinton now has a daughter.
(2) **Scott Hanf**[12]—married **Mary Mullen** and they had:
(i) **Stephanie Hanf**[13]
(ii) **Stephen Hanf**[13].
(3) **Lisa (Hanf) Thibault**[12]—married **Wayne Thibault** and they have one son:
(i) **Garron Thibault**[13].
(4) **Marilou (Hanf) Goreham**[12]—married **Vincent Goreham** and they had:
(i) **Rebecca Goreham**[13]
(ii) **Vincent Goreham, Jr.**[13]
(iii) **Kyle Goreham**[13].

2. **Sanford Harding**[11]—married **Eileen Kirkland** and they had:
(1) **Glenda Harding**[12]
(2) **Gayle Harding**[12]
(3) **Tracy Harding**[12]
(4) **Valerie Harding**[12].

3. **Gwennth (Harding) d'Eon**[11]—married **Paul d'Eon** and they had:
(1) **Ricky d'Eon**[12]
(2) **Randy d'Eon**[12]
(3) **Paul Joseph d'Eon**[12]
(4) **Patricia d'Eon**[12].

(by Victor) 4. **Bruce Cook**[11]—married **Barbara Owens** and they had:
(1) **Tammy Cook**[12]
(2) **Tina Cook**[12]
(3) **Angela Cook**[12]
(4) **Jennifer Cook**[12].

5. **Oren Cook**[11]—married 1st **Annette Doucette** and 2nd **Mary Roach.**
Oren and Annette had:
(1) **Marcia Cook**[12].

PHYLLIS BERNICE (RODGERSON) (HALEY) CHANDLER[10]

daughter of: Delcina (Perry) Rodgerson[9], Moses[8], Samuel[7], Levi[6], Moses[5], Samuel[4], Ezra[3], Ezra[2], Edmund[1].

MARRIED: 1st **William Haley** and 2nd **Mr. Chandler.**
CHILDREN: 1. **Curtis Haley**[11]—married **Sandra Ash** and they had:
(1) **Neil Haley**[12]
(2) **Crystal Haley**[12]
(3) a boy (name not known)
(4) a boy (name not known).

2. **Joy Haley**[11]
3. **Clark Haley**[11]
4. **Marsha (Haley) Warner**[11]—married **David Warner** and they had:
   (1) **Courtney Warner**[12].
   -information on the Rodgerson Family courtesy of Pauline Rodgerson

MATILDA 'TILLIE' (PERRY) NICKERSON[9]
daughter of : Moses[8], Samuel[7], Levi[6], Moses[5], Samuel[4], Ezra[3], Ezra[2], Edmund[1].

BORN: 15 December, 1888.
MARRIED: **Freeland Nickerson** (1880-1931). Freeland was 1st married **to Althea Ann Penney.**
DIED: October, 1956.
CHILDREN: 1. <u>**Elmer 'Barney' Nickerson**</u>[10]—born 1908; married **Ophelia Nickerson** (daughter of Bryon). Barney and Ophelia had at least 18 children.
2. **David Nickerson**[10]—born 1910; married 1st **Gladys Nickerson** (daughter of William). David and Gladys had three children:
   (1) **David Nickerson**[11]
   (2) **Joyce (Nickerson) Olie**[11]—married **Douglas Olie** from Windsor, Nova Scotia.
   (3) **William 'Billy' Nickerson**[11]—died from polio.
   David married 2nd **Edith Atkinson** and they had three children:
   (4) **Clinton Nickerson**[11]
   (5) **Bill Nickerson**[11]
   (6) **Harvey Nickerson**[11]
3. **Blanchard Nickerson**[10] —born 1912; died unmarried in 1936.
4. **Reta Parnell Nickerson**[10]—born in 1914; fatally burnt in 1919.
5. **Sarah (Nickerson) Scoville**[10]—born 1915; married **James Scoville**; divorced. James died in 1992. Sarah and James had one son:
   (1) **Rupert Scoville**[11]
6. **Alice (Nickerson) Ruse**[10]—born 1917; in 1942 married **John Ruse** of Winnipeg, Manitoba. John died in 1992.
7. **Harvey Nickerson**[10]—born in 3 July,1919; married **Penny Lindsay** from Alberta. Harvey died in 1977. Harvey and Penny had four children:
   (1) **Dana Nickerson**[11]
   (2) **Donald Nickerson**[11]
   (3) **Marcia Nickerson**[11]
   (4) **Kim Nickerson**[11]
8. <u>**Freeland 'Owen' Nickerson**</u>[10]—born 1921; in 1941, married **Mary L. Perry** (born 1921). Owen and Mary had 4 children:
   (1) **Louise Nickerson**[11]
   (2) **Loran Nickerson**[11]
   (3) **Lyle Nickerson**[11]
   (4) **Lee Nickerson**[11]

9. **Ellsworth 'Ellie' Nickerson**[10]—born in 1923; married **Gwendolyn Nickerson** (divorced). Ellie and Gwendolyn had 4 children:
   (1) **Ginny Alice Pauline (Nickerson) Wentzell**[11] —married **Robby George Wentzell** on 30 July, 1977. Ginny and Robby had one child:
      (i) **Amy Jean Alice Wentzell**[12]
   (2) **Gregory Nickerson**[11]
   (3) **Douglas Nickerson**[11]—married **Cathy Josey** (daughter of Alvin from Halifax).
   (4) **Deborah (Nickerson) Hamilton**[11]—married **Maurice Hamilton.**
10. **Elizabeth (Nickerson) McBain**[10]—born 1925; in 1943, married **Gilbert McBain.** Elizabeth and Gilbert had three children:
   (1) **Elizabeth McBain**[11]
   (2) **James McBain**[11]
   (3) **Nancy McBain**[11]
11. **Raymond Nickerson**[10] —born 1925; in 1952 married **Jean Gray** and moved to Saint John, New Brunswick. Raymond and Jean had four children:
   (1) **Keith Nickerson**[11]
   (2) **Karen Nickerson**[11]
   (3) **Katherine Nickerson**[11]
   (4) **Kevin Nickerson**[11]
12. **Edna (Nickerson) Gavel**[10]—born 1929; in 1955 married **Herman Gavel.** Edna and Herman had two children:
   (1) **Wayne Gavel**[11]—married **Ruth Rand** and they had three sons.
   (2) **Beverly (Gavel) Hoskisson**[11]—adopted; married **Lance Hoskisson** and they had three children:
      (i) **Alicia Hoskisson**[12]
      (ii) **Jennifer Hoskisson**[12]
      (iii) **Nicholle Hoskisson**[12]

ELMER 'BARNEY' NICKERSON[10]

son of : Matilda (Perry) Nickerson[9], Moses[8], Samuel[7], Levi[6], Moses[5], Samuel[4], Ezra[3], Ezra[2], Edmund[1].

BORN: 1908
MARRIED: **Ophelia Nickerson** (daughter of Byron) in 1934.
CHILDREN: 1. **Reta (Nickerson) Ball**[11]—married **George Ball.**
                  (1) **Laurie Ball**[12]
                  (2) **Kevin Ball**[12]
                  (3) **Cathy Ball**[12]
                  (4) a fourth child
              2. **Fred Nickerson**[11]—died in May, 1934.
              3. **Blanchard Nickerson**[11]—married **Beverly Lennox.** Blanchard and Beverly had 4 children:
                  (1) **Debbie Nickerson**[12]
                  (2) **Darlene Nickerson**[12]

(3) **David Nickerson**[12]
(4) **Daniel Nickerson**[12].
4. **Clifton Nickerson**[11]—married **Myrna Goodwin.**
 Clifton and Myrna had two children:
 (1) **Kim Nickerson**[12]
 (2) **Pam Nickerson**[12].
5. **Joyce (Nickerson) Walton**[11]—married **Albert Walton** and they had three children.
6. **Joseph Nickerson**[11]—married **Eleanor Goodwin.** Joseph and Eleanor had three children:
 (1) **Janet Nickerson**[12]
 (2) **Calvin Nickerson**[12].
 (3) **Gary Nickerson**[12].
7. **Ray Nickerson**[11]—married **Elaine Goodwin.** Ray and Elaine had two children:
 (1) **Dwayne Nickerson**[12].
 (2) **Crystal Nickerson**[12].
8. **Herbert Nickerson**[11]—married **Patricia Hurlburt** (daughter of Harold). Herbert and Patricia had two children:
 (1) **Ritchie Nickerson**[12]
 (2) **Shelley Nickerson**[12]
9. **Margaret (Nickerson) Hurlburt**[11]—married **Gerald Hurlburt** and they had two children:
 (1) **Cheryl Dawn Hurlburt**[12]
 (2) **Barry Leigh Hurlburt**[12]
10. **Owen Nickerson**[11]—married **Cora d'Entremont.** Owen and Cora had three children:
 (1) **Kelly Nickerson**[12]
 (2) **Melissa Nickerson**[12]
 (3) **Jeremiah Nickerson**[12]
11. **Wayne Nickerson**[11]—married **Maisie Nickerson** (daughter of Bradford). Wayne and Maisie had three children:
 (1) **Jason Nickerson**[12]
 (2) **Sonya Nickerson**[12].
 (3) **Bryon Nickerson**[12].
12. **Nancy (Nickerson) Quinlan**[11]—married **Charles Quinlan I.** Nancy and Charles had three children:
 (1) **Cory Quinlan**[12]
 (2) **Charles Quinlan II**[12]—died July, 1995.
 (3) **Curtis Quinlan**[12]
13. **Edith (Nickerson) Harris**[11]—married **Burke Harris.** Edith and Burke had two children:
 (1) **Colin Harris**[12]
 (2) **Tyler Harris**[12]
14. **William Nickerson**[11]—never married.
15. **Beverly (Nickerson) O'Connors**[11]—married **Rudolph O'Connors.** Beverly and Rudolph had three children:
 (1) **Rhonda O'Connors**[12]
 (2) **Randy O'Connors**[12]

(3) **Rodney O'Connors**[12].
16. **James Alfred Nickerson**[11]—married **Helena Ann D'Eon** in December, 1977. James and Helena had two children:
    (1) **Joshua Nickerson**[12]
    (2) **Darren Nickerson**[12]
17. **Patricia (Nickerson) McComiskey**[11]—married **Doward McComiskey** in December, 1977. Patricia and Doward had two children:
    (1) **Ryan McComiskey**[12]
    (2) **Gavin McComiskey**[12]
18. **Joyce (Nickerson) Watson**[11]—married **Albert Watson.** Joyce and Albert had four children:
    (1) **Heather Watson**[12]
    (2) **Nola Watson**[12]
    (3) **Brian Watson**[12]
    (4) **Adam Watson**[12]

FREELAND OWEN NICKERSON[10]

son of : Matilda (Perry) Nickerson[9], Moses[8], Samuel[7], Levi[6], Moses[5], Samuel[4], Ezra[3], Ezra[2], Edmund[1].

BORN: 1921
MARRIED: **Mary L. Perry** (born in 1921).
CHILDREN: 1. **Louise (Nickerson) Trask**[11]—married **Charles Trask** (son of Walter). Louise and Charles had 2 children:
            (1) **Charles Arnold Trask**[12]—married **Darlene Webb** on 12 November, 1983.
            (2) **Catherine (Nickerson) Elliot**[12]—married **Kevin Elliot.**
            2. **Loran Nickerson**[11]—married 1st **Cherlyn Wagner** in 1965. Loran and Cherlyn had 2 children:
            (1) **Lisa Nickerson**[12]
            (2) **Ronda Nickerson**[12]
Loran and Cherlyn were divorced in 1973, and Loran married 2nd **Loretta MacDonald** from British Columbia. Loran and Loretta had one child:
            (3) **Jason Nickerson**[12].
            3. **Lyle Nickerson**[11]—married **Cynthia Ann Robicheau** on 19 April,1977. Lyle and Cynthia had two children:
            (1) **Carly Nickerson**[12]
            (2) **Cory Nickerson**[12]
            4. **Lee Irving Nickerson**[11]—married **Pamela Lynn Trask** on 22 June,1985. Lee and Pamela had two children:
            (1) **Danielle Nickerson**[12]
            (2) **Dylin Nickerson**[12]

FRANCES (PERRY) SAULNIER[9]

daughter of :   Moses[8], Samuel[7], Levi[6], Moses[5], Samuel[4], Ezra[3], Ezra[2], Edmund[1].

BORN: in 1894 at Cape Negro, Shelburne County.
MARRIED: **Howard Saulnier**
DIED: 29 February, 1936.
CHILDREN: 1. **Clarence Albert Perry**[10]—born 22 May,1908 at Shag Harbour,
Shelburne County. He married **Dorothy Alma Reese** on 11
January, 1929. Dorothy Alma was born 4 September, 1906 in New
Ross, Lunenburg County, N.S. and she was the daughter of Alfred &
Alma (McDow) Reese. Clarence and Dorothy Alma had two children:
(1) **Eliza Alma 'Betty' (Perry) Boylen**[11]—born 17 April,1930;
married **Max Crandell Boylen** (son of Leonard & Joy
(Crandall) Boylen from Centreville, Kings Co., N.S).on 17 April,
1948. Betty and Max had three children:
(i) **Nancy Dale (Boylen) Eastman**[12] — (adopted); married
Wayne Eastman on 12 July,1972. Wayne died in a truck
accident on 31 July,1986. There were two children:
(a) **Tanya Dawn Eastman**[13]
(b) **Mark Eastman**[13]
(ii) **Lyle Maxwell Boylen**[12]—married **Annie Elizabeth Lewis**
on 28 October, 1987,(daughter of Gordon and Joan Lewis
originally from Digby County, N.S.) Lyle Maxwell and Annie
Elizabeth had three children:
(a) **Casey Elizabeth Boylen**[13].
(b) **Laura Maxine Boylen**[13]
(c) **Michael Lyle Boylen**[13]
(iii) **Lynda Grace (Boylen) Childs**[12] -married **Phillip Childs**
on 13 May, 1990.
(2) **Clarence St. Clair Perry**[11]—born 29 May, 1934; died 11
January,1942 in a car accident.
—*Information of the Perry-Boylen Family courtesy of Betty Boylen*

2. **Cynthia Amelia (Saulnier) (Wry) Shaw**[11]—born 1925; married 1st
Donald Wry and 2nd **Russell Shaw**. Cynthia died 18 March,1987.
Cynthia and Donald had:
(1) **Kenneth Wry**[12]—married **Margaret Deveau** on 19 October, 1968.
Kenneth and Margaret had one child:
(i) **Edward Wry**[13]
(2) **Ann Wry**[12]—died in infancy
(3) **Donna (Wry)(Pontney)(Smith)**[12]—Donna married 1st **Benjamin
Pontney** on 6 May, 1967.Donna and Benjamin had three children:
(i) **Betty Pontney**[13]
(ii) **Kevin Pontney**[13]
(iii) **Cindy Pontney**[13]
Donna married 2nd **James Smith** on 12 April, 1986.
(4) **Wayne Clarence Wry**[12]— married **Bonnie** on 13 June, 1970.
Wayne and Bonnie had one child:

(i) **Jonathan Wry**[13]

Cynthia married 2nd **Russell Shaw** and they had:

(5) **Michael Shaw**[12]

-information on the Wry Family courtesy of Wayne Wry

IDA MINERVA (PERRY) NICKERSON[9]

daughter of :   Moses[8], Samuel[7], Levi[6], Moses[5], Samuel[4], Ezra[3], Ezra[2], Edmund[1].

BORN: 1897

MARRIED: **Locksley Nickerson** (27 November, 1894- 5 October, 1963) from Shag Harbour, Nova Scotia in 1911.

DIED: 1965

CHILDREN: 1. male stillborn—27 September, 1912.
2. **Delilah Gertrude Nickerson**[10]—born 9 August, 1913; died in November, 1942; never married.
3. **Walter Burton Nickerson**[10]—born 1 September, 1915; died 28 June, 1958; never married.
4. **Cynthia Jane Nickerson**[10]—born 22 March, 1918; died 23 May,1918 of pneumonia.
5. **James Edwin Nickerson**[10]—born 19 August,1919; married **Bertha Louise Churchill**; died in December, 1978. James and Bertha had 8 children.
6. **Oran Eugene Nickerson**[10]—born 22 May, 1922; married 1st **Doris Irene Grand** (September, 1926 ,died July, 1958). Oran married 2nd **Rosemary Hopkins** . Oran fathered 7 children.
7. **Alden Murray Nickerson**[10]—born 16 February,1925; married **Goldie Pauline Waybret**. Alden and Goldie had 2 children:
   (1) **Gloria (Nickerson) Smith**[11]—married **Arthur Smith** and had:
      (i) **Bridgette (Smith) Dixon**[12]—born 1965; married **Terry Dixon**. Bridgette died 7 August, 1993. Bridgette and Terry had 2 children:
         (a) **Ryan Dixon**[13]
         (b) **Jerry Lynn Dixon**[13].
      (ii) **Bonnie (Smith) Banks**[12]—married **Troy Banks**. Bonnie and Troy had 2 children:
         (a) **Courtney Banks**[13]
         (b) **Kelsey Marie Banks**[13]
      (iii) **Gina (Smith) Ryer**[12]—married **Robert Ryer** and they had:
         (a) **Tristan Ryer**[13].
   (2) **Howard Alden Nickerson**[11]- born 1948; married **Lillian Lyll**. Howard died in 1975 . They had:
      (i) **Teresa Nickerson**[12]
      (ii) **Gidget Nickerson**[12]—born 1973 and died in 1991.
8. **Lindsay Alpheus Nickerson**[10]—born 28 June, 1929; married **Judith Atwood;** Lindsay died 24 April, 1982. Lindsay and Judith had 1 son:
   (1) **Lindsay Walter Nickerson**[11]—married **Linda Nickerson**.
9. **Layton James Nickerson**[10]—born 21 March,1932; married **Dorothy Banks** on 3 August 1956. Layton died 27 February,1995.

10. **Edna Minerva Nickerson**[10]—born 14 March, 1935; died November, 1935 of pneumonia.

11. **Gordon Alison Nickerson**[10]—married 1st **LaVerne De Mings**. Gordon and LaVerne were divorced and he married 2nd **Margaret MacKay**. Gordon and LaVerne had 2 children:

    (1) **Michael Nickerson**[11]—married **Carla Donaldson** and they had:

        (i) **Shana Nickerson**[12]

        (ii) **Chana Nickerson**[12].

    (2) **Alison (Nickerson) Smith**[11]—married **Kempton Smith** and had:

        (i) **Kayla Smith**[12]

        (ii) **Kyler Smith**[12]

        (iii) **Krista (Smith) Shand**[12]—married **Sandy Shand** and they had:

           (a) **Zachary Bradford Shand**[13]

12. **Mary Nickerson**[10]—died in infancy.

JAMES EDWIN NICKERSON[10]

son of: Ida (Perry) Nickerson[9], Moses[8], Samuel[7], Levi[6], Moses[5], Samuel[4], Ezra[3], Ezra[2,] Edmund[1].

BORN: 19 August, 1919
MARRIED: **Bertha Louise Churchill**
DIED: December 1978.
CHILDREN: 1. **Helen Marie (Nickerson) Nickerson**[11]—married **Frederick Nickerson** and they had:

    (1) **Wayne Nickerson**[12]—married **Susan Nickerson**.

    (2) **Clifford Nickerson**[12]

    (3) **Connie Nickerson**[12].

    2. **Gladys Barbara (Nickerson) Smith**[11]—married **John Smith** and they had:

    (1) **Wayne Smith**[12]

    (2) **Rickey Atwood Smith**[12]

    3. **Edna Louise (Nickerson) Nickerson**[11]—married **Donald Nickerson** and they have since divorced. Edna and Donald had:

    (1) **Dianna (Nickerson) Nickerson**[12]—married **Shawn Nickerson**. Dianna and Shawn had two children:

        (i) **Jonathan Nickerson II**[13]

        (ii) **Donovan Nickerson**[13].

    (2) **Jonathan Nickerson**[12]

    (3) **Tina Nickerson**[12]—Tina had one son:

        (i) **Chad Donald Nickerson**[13]

    4. **Blanchard Edwin Nickerson**[11]—married **Blanche d'Eon**. Blanchard and Blanche had:

    (1) **Bonnisa Nickerson**[12].

    (2) **Benjamin Nickerson**[12]

    (3) **Brian Nickerson**[12]

    5. **Bruce Clifford Nickerson**[11]—Bruce and his common-law wife, **Debbie Ryno**, had:

    (1) **Lisa Nickerson**[12]

    (2) **Angela Nickerson**[12]

(3) Cory Nickerson[12]
6. Calvin Merton Nickerson[11]—married **Dale Sears** and they had:
   (1) **Carrie Nickerson**[12].
   (2) **Melissa Nickerson**[12]
7. **Paulette Rose (Nickerson) Goreham**[11]—married **Morris Goreham**. Paulette and Morris have since divorced. Paulette and Morris had:
   (1) **Jamie Goreham**[12]—Jamie had a daughter:
      (i) **Jenna Ann Louise Goreham**[13]
   (2) **Loretta (Goreham) Smith**[12]—married **Darrell Smith**. Loretta and Darrell had:
      (i) **Dakota James Gary Smith**[13]
   (3) **Wanda Goreham**[12]—Wanda had a daughter:
      (i) **Rebecca May Goreham**[13]—
   (4) **Travis Goreham**[12]
8. **Alpheus Glendon Nickerson**[11]—married **Loretta Sears** and they had:
   (1) **Lori Nickerson**[12]
   (2) **Alan Nickerson**[12]
   (3) **Colin Nickerson**[12]

ORAN EUGENE NICKERSON[10]

son of: Ida (Perry) Nickerson[9], Moses[8], Samuel[7], Levi[6], Moses[5], Samuel[4], Ezra[3], Ezra[2], Edmund[1].

BORN: 22 May, 1922.
MARRIED: 1st **Doris Irene Grand** (Sept. 1926—July 1958); 2nd **Rosemary Hopkins**
CHILDREN: (by Doris)

1. **Robin James Nickerson**[11]—born 5 October,1944; married **Roselin Goodwin**. Robin died 8 October,1986. Robin and Roselin had:
   (1) **Ronald Nickerson**[12] —married **Jody Baker.**
   (2) **Shelley (Nickerson) d'Eon**[12]—married **Duaine d'Eon**.
      Shelley had 2 children:
      (i) **Shyla**[13]
      (ii) **Robin Tyler**[13]
2. **Russell Eugene Nickerson**[11]—married **Ethel Nickerson** and had:
   (1) **Nancy Nickerson**[12]
   (2) **Jill (Nickerson) Stoddard**[12]—married **Todd Stoddard** and had:
      (i) **Keigan Stoddard**[13]
      (ii) **Mikaela Olivia Stoddard**[13]
3. **David Arthur Nickerson**[11]—married **Sandra d'Entremont** and they had one adopted son:
   (1) **Tyler Nickerson**[12]
4. **Kendrick Michael Nickerson**[11]—married **Ethel d'Eon** and had:
   (1) **Mark Nickerson**[12]
   (2) **Joel Nickerson**[12]

5. **Ena Marie (Nickerson) Nickerson**[11]—married **Kenneth Nickerson** and they had:
    (1) **Nicholas Nickerson**[12]
6. **Burton John Nickerson**[11]—married **Bonnie Stoddard** and they had 2 children:
    (1) **Amanda Nickerson**[12]
    (2) **Terri-Gail Nickerson**[12]
(by Rosemary) 7. **Blake Anthony Nickerson**[11]

LAYTON JAMES NICKERSON[10]

son of: Ida (Perry) Nickerson[9], Moses[8], Samuel[7], Levi[6], Moses[5], Samuel[4], Ezra[3], Ezra[2], Edmund[1].

BORN: 21 March, 1932 in Shag Harbour
MARRIED: **Dorothy Banks**
DIED: 27 February, 1995 at Shag Harbour and is buried in Atwoods Brook Cemetery.
CHILDREN: 1. **Madeline (Nickerson) Crowell**[11]—married **Gordon Crowell**. Madeline and Gordon had 2 children:
    (1) **Michelle (Crowell) Dennis**[12] —married **Lionel Dennis** . Michelle and Lionel had 1 son:
      (i) **Gervais Dennis**[13].
    (2) **Amelia Crowell**[12.]
2. **Burnell 'Norman' Nickerson**[11]—married **Barbara Powers**.
3. **Stephen Nickerson**[11]—married **Laura Gore** and they had:
    (1) **Zacharic Nickerson**[12].
    (2) **Kaylee Nickerson**[12].
    (3) **Matthew Nickerson**[12].
4. **Jody Nickerson**[11]—married **Joy Crowell** and they had:
    (1) **Jordon Wayne Nickerson**[12].

Layton Nickerson's Obituary read:

Nickerson, Layton James—62, Shag Harour, Shelburne Co., died February 27, 1995, at Shag Harbour. Born in Shag Harbour, he was a son of the late Locksley and Ida (Perry) Nickerson. Surviving are his wife, the former Dorothy Banks; sons, Jody, South Side; Stephen, Woods Harbour; Norman, Shelburne; daughter, Madelene (Mrs. Gordon Crowell), Yarmouth; brothers, Alden, Gordon, Shag Harbour; Oren, Oak Park; six grandchildren; a great-grandson. He was predeceased by brothers, Edward, Walter, Lindsay; sisters, Gertie, Cynthia, Edna, Mary. Visitation 4-5, 7-9 p.m. today in H. Huskilson's Funeral Home, Barrington, where funeral will be 2 p.m. Wednesday, Pastor Luuk Geerligs officiating. Burial in Atwoods Brooks Cemetery. Donations to Heart and Stroke Foundation of Nova Scotia.

INDEX

115

BAIN

Charles Somner 29
Charlotte 25,26
Cheryl 36
Chester 38
Clara E. 31
Clarence 36
Clayton 37, 43
Conrad 33
Cora Lee 38
D. Lorraine 44
David R. 27
Dean 36
Deborah 31
Delancey 33
Donald 29
Doreen 30
Doris 27, 37
Dorothy J. 44
Douglas 35
Edgar 33, 36
Edna 43
Edward Edgar 32, 34
Egbert 29
Eleanor (1792) 23
Eleanor (1810) 22
Elijah 23
Elizabeth 43
Elizabeth Barbara 29
Elizabeth Louise 37
Elmer 33
Elsie 29
Emily Hannah 32
Emma 30,34
Enos Patten 32
Erma 38
Ernest F. 44
Ethel 45
Ethyle M. 28
Eugene 36
Eunice 22, 31, 32
Eva 34
Evelyn 36
Everett 43
Fanny 31
Fanny P. 38
Flora 43
Florence 44
Forrester 36
Frances 32, 34, 36, 38
Frederick 29, 33
Garfield 34
G. Clayton 29

George 29, 31, 33, 34, 35, 36
George St. Clare 35
George William 31
Georgia 29
Gerald 35
Gloria 36
Grant Ulysses 33
Harriet 38
Harriet (1803) 25
Harriet (1828) 27
Harriet E. 22, 28
Harold 36, 38
Harry 31, 43
Harry K. 29
Hasadiah 32, 34
Havileth 26
Havilla 28
Helen 30, 34, 35
Henry 34
Herman 34
Hilda 33
Howard 38
Howard B. 43
Hubert 29, 34
Ian 35
Ida 29
Irva 35
Irvin 35
Israel 37, 43
Israel L. 34, 37
Iva 34
Ivan 43
J. Natalie 44
Jacob 31
James 25, 34
James (1942) 30
James (1844) 31
James Brown 26, 28
James E. 38
James M. 28
James W. 28
Jean 36
Jennie 29
Jennie M. (1912) 45
Jenson Carol 38
Jeremiah 34
Jessica 45
Joan 29
John (1804) 22, 30
John E. (1781) 22
John J. 27
John Perry 32
John S. 30

116

BAIN

John William 34
Joseph 22
Joseph (1788) 23
Joseph (1843) 28
Joseph Patten 31
Joyce 35
Kathleen 36
Keith 36
Kenneth Ross 38
Larry 35
Laura 34
Leslie J. 35
Lillian 37
Lizzie 33
Lois 30, 37
Lois S. 32
Lloyd Nathan 27, 37
Margaret 29, 33, 44
Margaret E. 32
Maria 31
Maria Ellen 31
Marie 29
Marla 45
Martha 27
Martha (1837) 30
Mary 23
Mary 33, 34
Mary A. 28
Mary B. 26
Mary Anne 32
Mary Elizabeth 30
Matilda 30
Melitta Jane 37,38
Merle 27, 37
Michael 35
Mildred 29
Moses 26
Moses (1779) 22
Moses (1807) 25
Muriel 32
Murray S. 31
Nathan 45
Nathan (1870) 38, 44
Nathan S. (1908) 44
Nathaniel Patten 31
Nellie 29, 36
Norman B. 22, 32
Pauline 26
Percy 29, 38
Peter David St. Clair 37
Phyllis 36
Priscilla 34

Raymond 32, 36
Rebecca 25
Richard 32, 36
Rita Mae 32
Robert 33, 34, 37
Robert A. (1863) 38
Roger 37
Ronald St. Clair 37
Roxanna 23
Roy 36
Samuel (1785) 23, 30
Samuel (1831) 30
Samuel A. 31, 66, 67
Samuel Soames 22
Samuel Thorndyke 30, 32
Sarah (1783) 22
Sarah (1805) 25
Sarah (1837) 22
Sarah (1847) 28
Sarah A. 33
Sarah Agnes 29
Sophia 28, 31, 33
Sophia Killiam 32
Stafford Harrison 33
Stella 43
Stephen (1887) 27
Stephen (1889) 37
Stephen Perry (1893) 27, 38
Stephen Rose 32
Susan 26
Sydney 43
Thelma 29
Thomas 29
Tracy LaRae 37
Truman 38
Vincent 38
Wellesley 26
Wellesley (1841) 25
Wendell William 44
William 26, 27,32, 37
William (1787) 23,26, 33
William (1818) 31
Willis 36

BAKER

Alice 30
Edward 18
Enoch Vaughn 91
Hannah 63, 64
Hope 35

BREAKWELL
Candace 45

BRELAND
William Preston Jr. 100

BRIGHT
Christel Lee 42

BRITT
Daniel J. 98
James R. 97, 98
Janet L. 98
Jean A. 98
Sharon J. 98
Tammy J. 98
Thomas R. 98

BRIZET
Kenny 35
Marty 35
Maurice 35
Shelley 35

BRONSON
D.L. (Prof) 65

BROOKS
Julie Teresa 43

BROWN
Andrew Tyler 62
Bethia 22, 24
Burnett 28
Eleanor J. 71
Elizabeth 50, 51, 52
Elizabeth Miriam 62
George Duron 18
Jane 90
John 47
John Fremont II 62
John Fremont III 62
Joseph J. (Capt.) 47
Martha Susan 62
Mary Margaret 87, 88
Samuel 47

BRUMM
Alexander Kenneth Donald 42
David Charles 42
Donald Patrick 42
Katlyn Laura Marie 42
Kristopher Robert Grant 42

Stephen Aubrey Bruce 42
William 42

BRYNE
Robert 92

BUEHLING
Michelle Lynn 43

BURDOCK
John 94
John Evan 95
Sean Allen 94
Tracey Joanne 94

BURGESS
Brian 97
Crystal J. 97
Darlene Joyce 97
Deborah A. 97
Donna L. 97
Elizabeth 10
Ellis 97
Holly A. 97
Jeffery 97
Joshua 3
Justine 97
Michael J. 98
Nicholas D. 98
Patrick 97
Scott A. 98
Timothy J. 98

BURNS
Anna 51
Derek Scott 40
Hannah Jane 40

BURRELL
Caribel 50, 55

BURRIDGE
Clara Elizabeth 79, 80, 81

BURRILL
George H. 84

BURTON
Cora Belle 81

CHRISTIAN
Emily   45
Matthew   44
Michael   44
Sarah   44
Terrance   44

CHURCHILL
Annie R.   26
Bertha Louise   111, 112
Caroline C.   27
Edison   25
Eliza   59
Hazel Lillian   83
Herman   43
Sarah   59

CLARK
Sharon Gail   99

CLEMENTS
Alfred   70
Arthur Bain   41
Brenda Arlene   42
Daisy Gladys   40
David George   41
Dorothy Ann   42
Edwin   31
Elkanah   48
Errol Gilbert   41
Francis Pauline   41
George William   37, 38
Gilbert Ralph (Hon)   41
Glenda Ruth   41
Harvey G.   40
Janice Marion   41
John   47
John Kenneth   41
Jonah Robert Kenneth   41
Joseph B.   31
Julie Ann   41
Kenneth Stewart   41
Kristin Elizabeth Jean   41
Lizzie E.   39
Mabel S.   39
Mary Catherine   41
Mary Gail   41
Mary Janel Elaine   41
Mary Ruth Melitta   40
Nellie Jean   40
Pamela Colleen   41
Robert Kelly(1886)   40
Robert Kelly(1920)   40

Robert Kelly (1956)   41
Robert Steven   41
Silas (Capt) 6, 18, 73
Walter Leigh   41
William (1786)   47
William (1877)   39
William Leslie   41

CLEMO
Winona Mary   55

CLEVELAND
Patricia May   56

COBB
Mercy   17

CODY
Helen S.   77

COFFIN
Thelma Mary   41

COLLINS
Lois   17

COLPITTS
Marjorie   65
Merle   65
Mildred   65
Parker   65

COMEAU
Erin   102
Jamie Richard   103
Joyce Marion   103
Ken   102
Marilla   45
Richard B.   103
Terry   102

COOK
Alice   60
Angela   105
Bruce   105
Cynthia   89, 92
Ina Ethel   94
Jennifer   105
Manasseh   58
Marcia   105
Margaret   33
Marion   34
Oren   105

COOK
Sadie 66
Stephen 65
Susan 36
Tammy 105
Tina 105
Victor 102, 105
Walter 76

COOPER
James 49
Lloyd 68

COOSEY
Ethel May 51

CORCORAN
Myrtle 78, 79

COREY
Kim M. 97

CORNING
Adolphus 28
Augusta A. 28
Blanche Jean 96
Frank 28
Harold Arthur 94, 95
Hermie 28
John C. 29
Ida B. 28
Jennie L. 28
Joseph Walker 23
Mary 23
Mary Ann 95
Murray G. 28
Phoebe Elizabeth 77
Robert S. 28

COTTREAU
David Ambrose 96
Jonathan Robert 96
Leonard 90
Matthew Eugene 96

CRAWLEY
Tabitha 65

CREED
Winnifred Carol 41

CRITCHER
Hazel 56

CROCKER
Mary S. 51
Wendall (Capt.) 23

CROSBY
Alice 37
Anne 44
Annie 66
Anthony J. 77
Caleb Cook 76
Cornelius 66
Dawn 44
Emily Jane 76
Foster (Capt.) 76
Foster Stanton 76
Geoffery 44
George A. 76
Hannah Kelley 76
James Edgar 76
John B. (Capt.) 66
Jonathan 3
Knowles Eugene 30
Lemuel Staley 66
Louisa M. 77
Lynn 44
Margaret 63
Marietta A. 77
Marion 36
Martha 71
Mary A. 64
Mary D. 65
Nellie 36
Sarah Odessa 31
Thomas Allen 67
Thomas C. 66
Thomas P. 32
William 44

CROSS
Allan 90

CROSSMAN
Evelyn 57

CROWELL
Amelia 115
Annie 50
Forman 88
Gordon 114
Hallet (Capt.) 76
Joseph Hallett 49
Joy 114
Michelle 114

CROWELL
Sarah Betts 10

CUMMINGS
Lloyd 90

CUSHING
Edith 35
George (Capt.) 27

DALTON
Azor 24
Calvin 24
Harriet 24
Henry 24
Maria 24
Maurice 24
Melissa Jane 24

DANE
Norman J. 58

DAVIDSON
Effie 44

DAVIS
Ashley 79
Rebecca 79

DE MINGS
LaVerne 112

D'ENTREMONT
April 102
Charlene 102
Cora 108
Craig 102
Erica 95
Howard 95
Jules 102
Matthew 95
Sandra 113
Sarah 95
Vaughn 102

DECKER
Jean 90

DENNIS
Caroline 65, 67
Eunice 71
Gervais 114
Lionel 114

Sarah 63

DENTON
Ida 38
Martha 37, 43

D'EON
Blanche 112
Duaine 113
Ethel 113
Patricia 105
Paul 105
Paul Joseph 105
Randy 105
Ricky 105

DEVEAU
Margaret 110
Mark Daniel 104

DEXTOR
Angela 100
Gillian 101
Jerid 101
Kristen 101
Michael 100
Spencer 101
Traci 101

DEWOLFE
Charles (Capt.) 22,30

DILLION
John P. Jr. 97
Matthew John 97

DIXON
Jerry Lynn 111
Ryan 111
Terry 111

DOANE
Emery 89
Margaret 70
Marjorie 44

DODGE
Leah 23
Nancy 23
William 23

DONALDSON
Carla 112

GOODWIN
Eleanor 108
Grace 84
Mattie 29
Myrna 108
Nancy 82
Rebecca May 113
Roselin 114
Travis 113
Wanda 113

GORE
Laura 114

GOREHAM
Brennan Curtis Douglas 99
Jamie 113
Jenna Ann Louise 113
Jenna Michelle 99
Kyle 105
Loretta 113
Michael 99
Morris 113
Rebecca 105
Vincent 105

GOTTINGER
Caitlyn Elizabeth 55
Derek Michael 55
Jared Christian 55
Richard George 55

GOUDEY
Alice 26
Almira 30, 32
Ansel 26
Arthur 79
Elizabeth P. 23
George Russell 26
Grace 26
Harriet 22, 65
Henry 26
Jacariah 27
John 26
Joseph 26
Maurice 26
Myra 26
Nellie 79
Robert Azor 26
Stephen B. 26, 27
William 26
William Raymond 79

GRAND
Doris Irene 111, 113

GRANT
Olive 90

GRAVES
Penelope 98

GRAY
Mabel 36
Marshall 36
Stanley 28

GRAZULIS
Andrew 97
David 97
Rachel 97
Robert D. 97

GREENWOOD
Catherine Ann 89
Edith Lucille Joyce 94
Lorenzo 89, 99
Naomi 89
Seretha 89

GRESSETT
Blair Lee 43
Logan Michael 43
Michael Everett 43

GRICE
Thelma Kendall 91

GRISWOLD
Emery (Capt.) 75

GROSS
Deliverance 17

GUNNHILL
Anna Maria 23

HALEY
Clark 106
Crystal 105
Curtis 105
Elizabeth 18
Elizabeth Mary 71
Joy 106
Marsha 106
Neil 105

127

HOWELL
George   45
Malcolm   45
Sharon   45

HUGHES
Laura   69

HUMBER
Roselyn   104

HUME
Ashlee Margaret   41
Janice Courtney   41
Lindsay Marie   41
Mark Phillip   41

HUNTER
Elizabeth   22

HURLBURT
Ada   60, 61
April Marlene   82
Barry Leigh   108
Cheryl Dawn   108
Emma Maud   67
Gerald   108
Jerry Arthur   82
Melford   33
Patricia   108
Wallace   68

JOB
Judith Ann   70

JONES
Laura Elizabeth   98
Melissa Paige   98
Phillip   98
Phillip Thaine   98

JAYNE
Hailie   100

JEFFERY
Frank   37
James   37
Joseph   75

JENKINS
Anne   23
Jane   25, 27

JOHNSON
Annie Louisa   51
Daniel   63
George   58

JOHNSTON
William Wayne   79

JONES
Caroline   78
Mallory Elaine   40
Monica Ann   41
Robert Lee   40

JOSEY
Cathy   107

JUBIS
Christian   104
Michael David   104
Michael Ryan   104

KANE
Amanda   55
Christopher Lee   55
John   54
John David   54
Kyle   55
Michael Andrew   55
Noah   55
Zachary   55

KEAGLE
Jennifer Lynn   99
Matthew Wayne   99
Michelle Lee   99
Stephanie M.   99

KEENAN
Mary   28

KELLEY
Hannah   23, 30
Margaret   71
Muriel   69

KENNEDY
Margaret   76
Shaun   99

KENNEY
Ellen J.   81, 82
Mary Osborne   91

KILLIAM
Abraham 25
Jacob 25
Lois 25
Whitman 38

KILLIN
David James 43
Jennifer Elizabeth 43
Matthew Patrick 43
Michael Peter 43
Murray James 43
Nancy Louise 43
Paula Rayden 42
Peter George 43
Raymond John 40, 42
Robert John 43

KIMBALL
Hayford 70

KING
Ellen 63
Ina Maud 38,44

KINNEY
Lydia 50
Nathan (Capt.) 48

KIRBY
Christopher Frederick 95
David Christopher 95

KIRKLAND
Eileen 105

KLEINER
Anton 82
Evan Mark 82
Janice Elaine 82
Jordan Adam 83
Judith Ellen 82
Mark Anton 82
Ruth Anne Virginia 82
Wendi Marie 83

KNOX
Augusta 78

LAMB
Alice Dale 35
Anthony 35

LANDERS
Cynthia 75
Elisha Perry 75
Elizabeth 75
Eunice 23, 30
Joseph 87
Lois 34
Lois J. 87
Percy 43
Rachel 75
Samuel Perry 63
Sarah 22
Sealed 3, 6
Thankful 6
Thomas 75
Thorndyke 75
Zilpha 75

LANNIGAN
Neil 42

LARKIN
Margaret 38
Mayola 91

LAWRENCE
Ann Louise 57
Barbara Lorraine 57
Faith Margaret 57
Garet Blaine 82
Gordon 57
Lauren Aiel 82
Sandra Joyce 57
Sheridan 82

LAWTON
Anna 51
Charles L. 51
Harry 51
Jessie Evelyn 51
John 51

LEARY
Nellie 49

LEBLANC
Brian 105
Hazel "Madame" 44
Mary Celeste 102, 103
Quinton 105

LENNOX
Beverly 107

LEONARD
Sarah   10, 14

LEWIS
Annie Elizabeth   110
Nathan B.   25
Ruth Barnard   82

LIMBER
Sharon   37

LINDSAY
Penny   106

LLOYD
Douglas   70

LOCKE
Sarah MacLearn   25

LOCKWOOD
George   40
Henry Cecil   40
Kathleen Shirley   40, 42
Muriel Jean   40, 42
Patricia   55

LOVITT
Alexander Bain   23
Andrew   22
Annie M. Bolton   23
Henry   23
Israel   22
Joanna H.   25
John Walker   23
Joseph   23
Lydia Anne   23
Mary E.   23
Obadiah Wilson   23
Sarah   22
Thomas B.   22, 28

LYLL
Lillian   111

LYONS
Joseph Leigh   100
Joy Ann   100
Maxine Victoria   100
Ruth Elaine   92
Vivian   32

MABERLEY
Alexander Earl   82
Larry Alexander   82
Lawrence Earl   82
Melanie Dawn   82

MABEY
Jennie   79

MACCOY
Sarah   60

MACDONALD
Bessie   49
Blair   45
Bobbi Michelle   41
Brian Keith   41
Burton   45
Chad   45
Cyril Louis   41
Darren   45
Dorothy Faye   41
John Keith Luke   41
Katie   104
Loretta   109
Lori   104
Meaghan Brianne   41
Paul   104
Rachel Margaret   59
Scott Andrew 41
Shanna Colleen   41

MACGREGOR
Norman C.   28

MACKAY
Margaret   112

MACKENNA
Jonathan (Capt.)   24

MACKENZIE
Daniel   22
Kara   99

MACKERETH
Albert   68
Irene   68
Perry   68
Stanley   69
William W.   68

MACKINNON
John   21

MACMULLEN
George   58
Joseph W. (Capt.)   58

MACQUINN
Matilda   75

MACWILLIAMS
Thelma

MAGRAY
Andrew   58
Susanna   87

MAJOR
William   66

MALONE
Amanda Christine   83
Christopher Olin   83

MANN
Charles   55
Heather Margaret   55
Kathryn Louise   55
Sharon Elizabeth   55

MARLING
Barnet   75

MARKS
Dorothy Louise   62

MARSHALL
Dana Louise   103
Frank   103
Lynn   56
Peter   56
Samuel   76

MAUER
Nathaniel Boardman   62

MAXWELL
Sharon   98

MAZZEO
Elizabeth Simm   62
John   62

MCBAIN
Elizabeth   107
Gilbert   107
James   107
Nancy   107

MCCALLUM
Douglas   30
Sheila Dawn   30
Stewart Alan   30
William James   30

MCCLELLAND
Cameron James   96
Jennifer Jean   96
Michael Bruce   96
Patrick Michael   96

MCCOMISKEY
Doward   109
Gavin   109
Ryan   109

MCLAREN
Jill   79
Rick   79

MCLURE
Wilma Catherine   41

MCMULLIN
Kevin James   92
Nancy Ruth   92
Stephen   92

MCPHERSON
Alice Louise   99

MESSENGER
Samuel   19

MIDGLEY
Paul Edward   97

MILBURY
Louise   37

MILL
Phyllis   69

MILLER
Alice   88
Annie   66

NICKERSON

Avery Russell 90
Benjamin 112
Beverly 108
Bill 106
Blake Anthony 114
Blanchard 106, 107
Blanchard Erwin 112
Bonnisa 112
Brady 100
Brian 112
Bruce Clifford 112
Bryon 108
Burnell Norman 114
Burton Jon 114
Calvin 108
Calvin Merton 113
Carly 109
Carrie 113
Carrie Viola 70
Catherine 110
Chad Donald 112
Chana 112
Charles 101
Clifford 112
Clifton 108
Clinton 106
Colin 113
Connie 112
Cory 109, 112
Crystal 104, 108
Cynthia Jane 111
Dale 95
Dana 106
Daniel 108
Danielle 100, 109
Darlene 107
Darren 109
David 106, 108
David Arthur 113
Debbie 107
Deborah 107
Delilah Gertrude 111
Dianna 112
Donald 106, 112
Donna 95
Donovan 112
Doris Velma 56
Douglas 107
Dwayne 108
Dylin 109
Edith 108
Edna 107

Edna Louise 112
Edna Minerva 112
Elizabeth 107
Elizabeth May 70
Ellsworth 107
Elmer 106, 107
Ena Marie 114
Erdie 91
Ethel 114
Frank Melbourne 91
Fred 107
Fred H. 90
Frederick 112
Freeland 106
Freeland Owen 106, 109
Freeman 93
Gary 108
Gertrude 90
Gidget 111
Ginny Alice Pauline 107
Gladys 106
Gladys Barbara 112
Gloria 111
Gloria Viola 90
Gordon Alison 112
Gordon Arnold 70
Gregory 107
Gwendolyn 107
Harvey 106
Helen Marie 112
Herbert 108
Howard Alden 111
Howard Woodman 90
James Alfred 109
James Edwin 111, 112
Janet 108
Jason 108, 109
Jeremiah 108
Jill 113
Jody 114
Joel 113
Jonathan 112
Jordon Wayne 114
Joseph 108
Joshua 109
Joyce 106, 108, 109
Justin 104
Karen 107
Kassidy 100
Katherine 107
Kayla 100
Kaylee 114
Keith 107

O'ROURKE
Daniel 57
Michael 57
Peter 57
Sean 57

OWENS
Barbara 105

PACEY
Winnifred 52

PALMER
Beatrice E. 97
Edward 29
Ernestine 44
Faye L. 97
Francine L. 97
Freda 29
Frederick R. 97
Joyce 97
Raymond Chesley 94, 97
Thelma 29
Wilbur 29

PARR
Lady Margery 7

PATTEN
Benjamin P. 32
Lydia Ann 31
Mary 31
Sarah Crosby 31

PATTERSON
Brenda Eileen 40
Harriet 66
Linda Marlene 40
Malcolm Grenville 40
Melda Elaine 40

PEARL
Jessie 32

PENCHARD
Florence 45
George 45
Marie 45

PENNEY
Althea Ann 93, 106

PERRY
Abigail 58, 63, 75, 76,77
Abigail Dennis 69
Adelbert 60
Alan Ramsay 70
Albert Booth 50
Albert Vandella 68
Albert William 91, 92
Alfred 75, 77
Alfred Lawrence 59
Alice 65
Alice Jane 67
Alice Sophia 81
Almira 58
Alva 65
Alvin (1870) 60
Alvin Ernest 69
Amanda 76
Amasa Durkee 49
Amos S. 78
Amy C. 65
Andrew Scott 82
Anna (1761) 5,6, 10, 73
Anna (1789) 75
Anna Foster 84
Anna Marguerite 52, 53, 54
Anna Maria 50, 51
Anna R. 67
Anne 66
Annie Althea 94, 98
Annie E. 78
Ansel 24
Arnold John 79
Arnold V. 67
Arthur 6
Arthur Franklin (1866) 68
Arthur Franklin II 68
Avery Dean 90
Avery Palmer 90
Bahji 91
Balfour St. Clair 69
Barbara 89
Benjamin 75
Bernard W. 65
Bernice 90
Bertha 59
Bertha Annie 85
Bertha Laurena 50
Bertha Maude 81
Beulah 78
Blanche Burton 81
Blanche Lillian 68

PERRY

Faith Marinda Ann 101
Farwell 64
Flora Blanche 51
Florence 67
Florence Evangeline (Dr.) 80
Florence Stella 81
Foster 75
Foster (1839) 60
Frances 93, 110
Frank 58
Frank Chester 51
Frank D'Arcy 77
Frank Lyman 50
Franklin Leslie 89
Frederick Hammond 76, 81, 85
Frederick Manasseh Clinton 94
Frederick Russell 69
Frederick Tompkin (Capt.) 67, 68
Freeman James 67, 69
Garrett Wayne 101
Gary Marshall 99
Gayle 79
George 75, 78
George Fred (Rev.) 94, 99
George Gordon 60
George H. 78, 79
George Hay (Capt.) 77, 79
George Henry (Capt.) 79, 80
George Henry (1841) 84
George Herman 81
George Stanley 77
Georgina 61
Gertrude 84
Gladys D. 90
Gladys Cook 94, 97
Gordon 31, 78, 90
Grace 59
Graham 31
Hannah (1829) 65, 87
Hanson Philbrooke 91
Harley Edon 69
Harriet H. 76
Helen Catherine 70
Helen M. 77
Helen Minerva 81
Helen Sophia 76, 81, 85
Helena 78
Henrietta 58
Henry (Henrici) 7, 10
Henry Heckman 52, 53
Henry Strawn 68
Herbert Leslie 91

Hiram 75
Hope 91
Ida Cleveland 69
Ida May 60, 85
Ida Minerva(1897) 93, 111
Ileta Annie 92
Ina 90
Isabella 65
Isabelle Beatrice 81
Jackie George 99
James (1825) 65
James (1835) 66
James Albert 50, 77, 78, 84
James Alfred 78
James Douglas 83
James Forman 84
James Levi 92
James William 49, 77
Jane Alice 100
Jane Diane 52
Janet Horton 49
Janice 79
Jean 55, 57
Jean Viola 94, 95
Jessie May 81
Joanna Collins 17
Joel 66
John (1788) 47, 58
John (1818) 64
John (1824) 58
John (1842) 64, 89
John (1872) 84
John (1903) 78
John H. 89
John Harold 100
John Lockhart 58
John M. 64
John MaGray 87
John W. (1828) 84
Jonathan 64
Jonathan Osborne 69
Joseph 90
Joseph (1756) 10, 20
Joseph (1781) 47
Joseph (Capt.) (1800) 48, 49
Joseph Evelyn 49
Joseph Foster 84
Josephine 78
Julie 58
Justin Walter Arthur 83
Kenneth Milton 59
Krista Danielle 83
Lahiah 32

PERRY

Laliah 64
Laurier Raymond 80
Lawrence Chester 81, 82
Lawrence Wentworth 51, 57
Leigh Ann 99
Leland 90
Lemuel Wilmont 78
Lena Viola 90
Leonard (1798) 76, 81
Leonard (1878) 84
Leonard Ray 51
Leonard William 67
Leonora F. 49
Leslie 91
Leslie Bloomfield 59
Leslie Wayne 94, 101
Levi (1766) 5, 10, 87
Levi (1839) 89
Lewis Alan 69
Lillian 59
Linda 57
Lizzie L. 60
Lloyd Franklin 90
Lockhart 61
Lois Emily 50
Loisa 17
Lorne Cameron 52
Louisa 60
Louisa Marguerite 52
Lucinda 76
Lydia 50
Lydia (1788) 63
Lydia (1821) 65, 66
Lydia (1843) 89
Lydia Ellen 50
Lydia S. 84
Mabel B. 67
Maebel Adelaide 77
Maiben Aird 52, 53, 54
Margaret 75
Margaret (1895) 70
Margaret A. 89
Margaret J. 49
Margaret Veda 94, 101
Margaret Winifred 81
Margery J. 58
Maria (1832) 59
Maria Agnes 51
Marianne Elaine 92
Marion Ann 79
Marion Caroline 70
Martha (1840) 66

Martha Huntington 84
Martha M. (1857) 59
Martha May 60, 85
Mary 65
Mary (1798) 63
Mary Agnes 51
Mary Ann 87
Mary Bertha 90
Mary Booth 50
Mary E. (1834) 66
Mary E.(1865) 49
Mary Jane 78
Mary L. 106, 109
Mary Polly 47
Matilda 93, 106
Matthew 101
May 91
Medley Thomas 77
Melvin 59
Michael Hanson 91
Mildred Ernesta 90
Minnie 78
Molly Polly 47
Monica Dawn 83
Moses (1714) 3, 4, 5, 10, 15, 16
Moses (1752) 10, 19
Moses (1787) 17
Moses (1794) 87
Moses (1846) 89, 93
Moses Ellis (1819) 17
Muriel 90
Muriel Lucille 81
Murray L. 49
Nathan 65, 67
Nathan Douglas 67
Nathan Gordon 51
Nathan Kinney 50
Nathan Maurice 69
Nathaniel (1759) 10, 63
Nathaniel (1791) 63, 64
Nathaniel (Capt.) (1819) 65
Nehemiah Clements 51
Nehemiah Ernest 50
Nettie W. 67
Nita Joyce 64
Norah Alice 79
Norman J. 65
Oliver P. 76
Patricia Antoinette 70
Paul Russell 79
Penelope Alice 99
Perry Ellen 81
Philbrooke Osborne 91

PERRY

Philip Thomas 83
Phillip Carleton 69
Phoebe Ann 89
Phyllis 91
Prence 10, 17
Prince William (Capt.) 50
Rachel Dorothy 91
Ralph 60
Raymond 90
Raymond Alan 57
Rebecca 84
Rebecca (1748) 10, 17, 73
Rebecca (1794) 63, 71
Rebecca (1831) 65
Robert Charles (Capt.) 51
Robert Ernest 51
Robert Walter (Dr.) 83
Robin Leslie 99
Rodney Clinton 99
Rodolph 79
Ronald Frederick 82
Rosalie Joyce 92
Rosalie Ruth 83
Roscoe 78
Ross Webster 49
Rowland Briggs 87
Roy C. 67
Rufus 75, 77
Russell 78, 79
Ruth 17
Ruth Armintha 91
Ruth Ellen 49
Ruth H. 76
Sadie M. 65
Samuel (1687) 10, 14
Samuel (1769) 10, 20
Samuel Albert 90
Samuel (Capt.)(1827) 65
Samuel James 87, 88
Sanford 93
Sarah 65, 89
Sarah (1750) 10, 21
Sarah (1764) 75
Sarah (1791) 75
Sarah (1797) 63
Sarah Anne (1804) 48, 75
Sarah Emma (1832) 65
Seretha Ada 79
Seretha Hazel 79
Sophia Walker 84
Sophronia 75, 76
Staley 60

Stephen 64
Stephen C. 70
Susan Marie 83
Susannah 87
Sylvanus 84
Sylvanus B. 85
Tammie Lee 99
Tanya Lynn 99
Terrance 90
Thomas (1755) 10, 47, 48
Thomas (1779) 47, 48
Thomas (1804) 76, 84
Thomas (1823)(Capt.) 50, 51,52, 53
Thomas (Capt)(1832) 59
Thomas (1852) 64
Thomas (1854) 64
Thomas (1874) 84
Thomas Donald 52
Thomas Henry 83
Thomas James (Capt.) (1832) 49
Thomas Raymond 57
Thomas William 77
Timothy 101
Todd Christopher 100
Trevor Daniel 83
Vera Genevieve 68
Verna Louise 60, 85
Violet May 68
Virginia Helen 82
Wade Alvin 83
Walter 5
Walter Emerson 82
Wayne 90
Wellington Whitfield (Capt.) 60, 85
Wentworth Kinney 51
W. Eva 65
Wilfred Ernest 92
William (1786) 47
William (1845) 64
William Albert 67
William Edgar 60
William Edward 50, 55
William H. 59
William Horton 49
William Nelson 76
William Robbins 69
Winnifred Ethel 94, 95
Zipha 76

PERRYE

Henry (Henrici) 8, 9
Richard 7
Roger 7

140

ROBERTS
Jack 61

ROBERTSON
William 23

ROBICHEAU
Cynthia Ann 109
Emily Mary 82

RODGERSON
Alex 104
Alexandra 104
Alvin 102
April 103
Blaine 102
Brian 102
Carolyn 102
Carrie 104
Cecil 103
Chrissie 103
Constance Elaine 104
Cory 104
Curtis Nicholas 104
Curtis Russell 104
David 104
Donald Bruce 104
Elaine Anne 104
Elizabeth Ann 101
George Russell 104
Helen Esther 101
Holly Marie 104
James Robert 104
Joan 102
John 102
John Alvin 102
John Brian 104
John Henry 93, 101
Jordon Troy 103
Joseph David 104
Joyce 102
Judith Ann Linda 104
Judy 102
Kelly 104
Kenny 102
Lance Kenneth LeRoy 103
LeRoy Ralph 103
Lorraine 102
Marc Eric 104
Marilyn 102
Mary Edna 102, 105
Melissa 104
Nellie Vingenetta 103

Oren Burton 101
Pamela Lee 103
Paul 104
Phyllis Bernice 102, 105
Ralph LeRoy 102, 103
Randy 102
Russell Clifton 102, 103
Sanford Eugene 101
Sharon Ann 104
Shelley Marie 104
Sherry Anne 103
Stuart 104
Tammy 102
Terry 102
Theresa Darlene 104
Troy Lee William 103
Wanda Marie 104
William Stuart 104

RODNEY
Alice 26
Harriet Cynthia 32
Hugh 43

ROGERS
Bessie 49
Dorothy 102
Douglas 49
Edna 49
Israel L. 49
J. Lovitt 49
Thomas 34

ROSE
David 28
George M. 64
George W. 28
Henry 28
Hope 35
Laura 28
Lois 28
Martha 24, 27
William B. 34
Zella Mary 83

ROSS
Mansfield 80, 81

RULMON
Colonel Christian 19

RUSE
John 106

143

SMITH
Bridgette 111
Clarissa 65
Dennis Morton 98
Donna Charlotte 100
Eliza J. 58
Ella Maude 94
Emery Douglas 98
Ethel Mildred 95
Frank 67
Gina 111
Hannah 58
Hazel Amanda 98
Herman Leland 94
Howard J. 58
Irene Elaine 98
James 65, 110
Jeremy Andrew 99
Joel Munroe 65
John 112
Joseph 33
Joy Gail 99
Kayla 112
Kempton 112
Krista 112
Kyler 112
Leslie Stanford 94, 98
Lucy A. 58
Maria K. 58
Maynard 94, 100
Mercy 87
Monty Emery 98
Morton (1976) 95
Morton Leslie 98
Nancy Louise 98
Paul 95
Ricky Atwood 112
Samantha 95
Shannon Monty 99
Stacy 95
Thomas P. 58
Todd 103
Travis Leslie Douglas 99
Wayne 112

SMITHERS
John 84

SNOW
Irving 89
Isabel 91

SPICER
Roland 29

SPINNEY
Ethel 66

STALKER
John 89

STANWOOD
Ada 26
Charles Tooker 26
Effie P. 26
Enoch (Capt.) 26
George W. 26
Joseph (Capt.) 24
Samuel F. 26

STEADMAN
William 76

STEELE
Aminilla 51
John 32
Laura J. 97

STEEVES
Samantha Ashley 82

STERRITT
James A. (Capt.) 47

STEVENS
Goldie 43

STEWART
David 35
Mary Ruth 40

STODDARD
Bonnie 114
Keigan 113
Mikaela Olivia 113
Todd 113

STOWE
Edith 76
Larry Michael 100

STRANG
Kenneth 90